C000162267

RUN
PARTNERSHIP

RUNNING A PARTNERSHIP

Margaret Richards

Director of Training, Eversheds Hepworth & Chadwick

Ian Richardson

Partner, Eversheds Hepworth & Chadwick

JORDANS

1993

Published by
Jordan Publishing Limited
21 St Thomas Street
Bristol BS1 6JS

British Library Cataloguing-in-Publication Data

A catalogue record for this book is available from the British Library.

ISBN 0 85308 172 7

Photoset by Rowland Phototypesetting Ltd, Bury St Edmunds, Suffolk
Printed by Henry Ling Ltd, The Dorset Press, Dorchester

Preface

Partnership as a business medium was designed for the Victorian era, when enterprises were smaller and commercial engagements less regulated than they are today. The unlimited liability of a partner to a client or customer for the obligations of the firm was part of that culture, but the Partnership Act 1890 also provides a broad enabling framework within which partnerships may regulate their own internal affairs. The contrast between what is still the primary source of partnership law and the far more detailed regulation of the management of limited companies could not be more marked.

It is remarkable that the law has not altered significantly in the last hundred years, and that partnership remains a viable concept, however large the firm and albeit cloaked in a corporate veneer. The attraction is perhaps that the relationship can be moulded to suit the particular needs of the individual business and of the people running that business.

This book is intended for partners in professional firms, as a practical guide to the nature of their legal relationship with each other and with the outside world. Our experience, as legal advisers in disputes between partners, has made us aware of the importance of a well-drafted and comprehensive partnership agreement. Consequently, we have sought to emphasise throughout the book how the Partnership Act 1890 encourages firms to regulate their own internal affairs via the partnership agreement, and have made detailed suggestions as to what should go into such agreements.

The book has a star-rating system which indicates the degree of need to take professional advice. One star means advice is desirable; two stars means it is recommended; and three stars means it is essential. For partnerships, it is likely to be essential above all to take advice on the contents and drafting of the partnership agreement, and Chapter 3 sets out a detailed agenda for discussion with the firm's legal advisers. Chapter 10 looks more generally at a firm's potential need for professional advice other than from lawyers and suggests how to get the most out of using such professionals.

Thanks are due to the many colleagues who have contributed their ideas to this book. First and foremost we would like to acknowledge the contribution of Sarah Lane, lecturer in law at the University of Leeds and part-time consultant to Eversheds Hepworth & Chadwick, who wrote Chapter 7 on partnership tax and commented on the manuscript as a whole. We are also indebted to Charles Clement, formerly of Ernst Young, and Tim Hague of Berkeley Jackson, both of whom gave us valuable assistance with the chapter on partnership accounts. Thanks also to Pervez Ahktar, James Coley, Daniel Weston and Peter Wordsworth who researched various sections of the book, and to Geraldine

Smith who processed and reprocessed the drafts of the original manuscript. Any errors or omissions are, of course, entirely our responsibility.

MARGARET RICHARDS
IAN RICHARDSON
Leeds
October 1993

Contents

CHAPTER 1

What is a Partnership?

INTRODUCTION

'Partnership', 'firm', 'business', 'company' – in everyday language we tend to use these terms indiscriminately to refer to various kinds of commercial or professional undertakings. In fact, they all have different legal meanings and it is important to be aware of these, mainly because misunderstandings can otherwise easily occur, possibly with adverse financial consequences.

A partnership is a legal relationship between individuals engaged in a professional commercial enterprise. A partnership does not have a separate legal identity. Strictly speaking, the whole is no more than the sum of the parts, and 'partnership' is just a collective noun. A partnership cannot make contracts with people, employ people, or commit crimes – only the partners can. To this extent the social partnership created by marriage has an identical legal nature.

A company, by contrast, is a separate and independent legal person which can incur rights and liabilities in the same way as an individual can. So the company itself will enter into business agreements with outsiders, and the company itself will employ its staff.

In Chapter 12 there is a more detailed discussion of the essential differences between a partnership and a limited company, and of the factors which may influence the choice of business medium and, ultimately, the decision whether or not to incorporate. For many professional partnerships, of course, incorporation is not an option, as we shall see.

THE LEGAL DEFINITION OF A PARTNERSHIP

The backbone of partnership law is the Partnership Act 1890 ('the 1890 Act'). Microchips, FAX machines and satellite communication notwithstanding, we still apply a Victorian statute to commercial relationships in the 1990s!

The 1890 Act states that a partnership is 'the relation which subsists between persons carrying on a business in common with a view of profit'. This definition is outwardly simple; the words used are a far cry from the complex drafting of modern statutes, eg the Companies Act 1989. We shall see, however, that every word counts, and simplicity may be deceptive.

'The relation'

The 1890 Act makes clear that a partnership is a legal relationship between individuals, and no more than that. This means that a person who enters into an agreement with a partnership which uses, for example, the name 'Eversheds Hepworth & Chadwick', will be conducting a legal relationship not with any entity called Eversheds Hepworth & Chadwick, but with the partners in Eversheds Hepworth & Chadwick. The fact that they are partners, and not merely friends or colleagues, also means that any one partner is able to make agreements on behalf of his fellow partners and is equally bound to carry out agreements made by them. Technically, each partner has personal unlimited liability for any partnership debt, and this is capable of extending to all that partner's assets, including his home and his personal investments. The nature of a partner's liability for partnership obligations is discussed further in Chapter 4.

Comparison with a limited company

The position of an individual ('A') contracting with a limited company ('X Ltd') is essentially different. Since incorporation means that a company is a legal entity quite distinct from its shareholders, the legal relationship which is effected will be directly between A and X Ltd. The shareholders in X Ltd will not be part of that legal relationship and will owe no duties to A.

Admittedly, however, this distinction may become blurred in practice, because banks and others who lend money to limited companies will often require personal guarantees of repayment from the directors and shareholders, who consequently may become liable as individuals for the debts of their company to the full extent of their personal assets, in very much the same way as partners are.

'Persons'

Although the suggestion is that a partnership can only exist between human beings, that is not wholly true. A partnership between limited companies is possible – perhaps in the context of a joint venture – as is a partnership between limited companies and individuals. Young people under the age of 18 are 'persons' and so may be partners, although this is inadvisable because they do not have the capacity to incur binding legal obligations to partners or to anyone else. The legal disabilities which used to attach to married women disappeared long ago, but partnerships between spouses or cohabitants may still give rise to particular difficulties. These are considered in Chapter 11.

'Business'

The 1890 Act defines 'business' as including every trade, occupation, or profession. Essentially, therefore, there must be some commercial venture, eg selling goods or services for reward, before a partnership can exist. It now seems to be accepted that a one-off enterprise can be constituted as a partnership, but the fact remains that not all profitable activities can be regarded as businesses. The 1890 Act itself makes this clear by stating that joint ownership of land or other property does not, of itself, create a partnership in that property.

Carried on 'in common'

One occasionally sees the phrase 'sole partner' on a letter heading. This is a contradiction in terms, since a partnership requires the involvement of at least two people in the business. However, such involvement may be active or passive. The courts have held, for example, that a partnership will exist where a business is run by one or more persons on behalf of themselves and others, so introducing the notion of a 'sleeping' partner.

'With a view of profit'

This aspect of the definition distinguishes partnerships from social enterprises like members' clubs or voluntary associations and from mutual insurance societies. The purpose of a partnership is to make profits, and without this essential aim a partnership cannot exist in law. At one time it was considered necessary for a partnership to be set up not only to make profits but to divide them. However, the 1890 Act no longer requires this, so that a partnership can exist with the object of making profits for charity rather than for the personal benefit of the partners. In the same way, an agreement between individuals to share losses as well as profits will be strong evidence of the existence of a partnership (see p 6).

BEGINNINGS

Partnership is like marriage; easy to get into, hard to get out of without discomfort. That is why it is essential to be able to identify the precise moment at which a partnership comes into existence. The important point is that, unlike marriages, partnerships can occur informally or even inadvertently, when none of the individuals involved intends or anticipates this consequence.

Whether or not a partnership exists is a legal question. If the essential ingredients of the definition discussed above are, in fact, present, a partnership will exist, whatever the individuals themselves may intend. From that moment the 1890 Act will regulate legal relations between the partners and the outside world, as described in Chapter 4 below. At the same time, so far as the relationship between partners is concerned, the 1890 Act is essentially a voluntary code. This means that if partners and would-be partners are prepared to anticipate the consequences of their own relationship and regulate it themselves, the courts will not generally interfere.

The moral, for such people, is clear: think about the way you and your partners wish to run your business; plan ahead; and use the law pro-actively by seeking professional advice before committing yourself to a commercial venture.

In some circumstances, however, the existence, or otherwise, of a partnership may be a source of dispute. In this situation the question will be: how is it possible to distinguish partnerships from other relationships which appear to be rather similar?

Questions like this are likely to arise in three main circumstances:

(1) where someone who has dealt with a firm seeks to make another person, not his immediate contact, liable for a debt on the basis that he is a partner in the firm. The point is crucial because if that other person is not a partner, he will not be liable;

(2) where someone seeks to enforce an obligation from another person on the basis that they are partners with each other, and consequently owe such obligations to one another;

(3) where tax payers are seeking to establish the existence of a partnership because it will be advantageous for tax purposes.

It will be apparent that disputes as to the existence of a partnership may focus on whether an individual is a partner or an employee, or whether he is a partner or a creditor. To resolve such questions the person who wishes to rely on the existence of a partnership will have to convince the court, or the Inland Revenue, that it does, in fact, exist.

The test of partnership

Whether or not a partnership exists has to be determined by reference to the substance of the relationship between the alleged partners. An agreement between individuals that they are partners may not be conclusive if their actions indicate that they are not.

Nowadays, the majority of partnerships are entered into in a careful and considered way, and there will usually be a formal partnership agreement (see Chapter 3). In such cases, the intention to create a partnership clearly accords with the acts of the would-be partners. However, even in cases like these the courts have frequently said that individuals cannot create a partnership simply by saying that there is one. In particular, if the court gets involved in a dispute over the existence of a partnership, it will want to know what actually happened and not simply what was agreed should happen, and when the partners actually started to carry on the business, not just the 'official' starting date shown in the partnership agreement itself. These are points which need to be considered when drawing up a partnership agreement, particularly where the agreement itself is being prepared *after* the parties to it consider that the partnership itself came into existence.

Not all would-be partners prepare formal partnership agreements; nor, significantly, do individuals who enter into business transactions without thought as to whether they are, or would wish to be, partners. In such circumstances, there are guidelines laid down in the 1890 Act to help define whether or not a partnership exists.

(1) JOINTLY OWNED PROPERTY

Where two or more individuals own property jointly they will not be partners for this reason alone, even if they share profits made by the use of the property. So, for instance, if X and Y agree to buy a case of wine between them, because that is cheaper than buying six bottles each, and X is responsible for ordering the wine, but fails to pay for it, the supplier will not necessarily be able to recover the cost from Y on the basis that a partnership exists. If, on the other hand, the intention was to resell the wine at a profit, the business relationship essential to partnership would exist, and there would be joint, and unlimited, liability. Thus, the supplier would be able to recover the money owed from Y.

(2) SHARING PROFITS

The sharing of net profits (after tax and expenses) is strong evidence that a partnership exists. However, sharing the gross receipts of a business will not signify a partnership and, in certain circumstances, neither will profit-sharing. Examples where profit-sharing will not, necessarily, constitute a partnership are:

- agreeing to pay an employee a share of the profits as part of his remuneration package;
- paying the widow or child of a partner who has died a share in the firm's profits by way of an annuity;

– repaying a creditor by instalments out of profits, or paying him a rate of interest which is determined by the size of the profits. (For further discussion on lending money to a partnership, see Chapter 11);

– selling a business in which the vendor is paid by reference to future profits.

If, however, there is an arrangement to share losses as well as profits, that will usually be conclusive evidence of the existence of a partnership. The reason for this is that sharing losses signifies acceptance of risk and, therefore, indicates that the individual who has agreed to do this is truly participating in the business.

LEGAL CONTROLS ON PARTNERSHIPS

Partnerships, in the main, are less heavily regulated by the state than are limited companies, and this may sometimes make a partnership a preferable vehicle for carrying on a business enterprise. There are, however, areas where the public interest does require limits to be placed on partnership activities, and these are outlined as follows.

The name

The true collective term for partners, both commercially and legally, is 'a firm'. For marketing purposes, a firm may adopt a name which does not coincide with the names of the partners. Legally, such a name will be superfluous in that it cannot give the firm a separate legal identity, and it will not alter the basic position that each partner is liable to the full extent of his personal assets to any creditor of the firm. Nevertheless, the adoption of a particular name can cause problems for the partners if it is 'too like' the name of another firm, to the extent that clients or customers may be misled. In such circumstances, the first firm to trade under a particular name or title can protect itself, by a court action for 'passing off'.

Subject to the above, a firm is generally at liberty to adopt any name it considers will identify the firm sufficiently to promote its business.

However, the Business Names Act 1985 imposes certain limitations for the benefit of customers or clients of the firm. It requires that any business name which does not consist only of the surnames of all individual partners must be approved by the Secretary of State for Trade and Industry. This rule will affect any sizeable partnership, plus any firm which uses a trade name rather than the surnames of its partners.

In addition, certain words or expressions which are incorporated into business names are required to be approved. Some have to be approved by the Secretary of State, for example 'insurance', 'register', 'chemist' and 'trust'. In other cases, the owner of the business must seek the approval of certain other bodies, and satisfy the Secretary of State that this has been done. For example, use of the phrase 'health centre' will require the approval of the Department of Health and use of the word 'dental', or 'dentistry' will require the approval of the General Dental Council. A complete list of all these requirements is set out in Appendix 1. It should also be noted that the use of certain words by professional firms may be subject to professional control. For example, the designation 'architect' is limited to those people who are registered as such under the Architects (Registration) Act 1931. In cases of doubt, confirmation should be sought from the appropriate professional body. A list of terms which are subject to professional control in this way can also be found in Appendix 1, together with a list of the professional bodies from whom advice may be sought.

The Business Names Act 1985 provides that a partnership must disclose the name and address of each partner on all its business documents (letters, orders, receipts, invoices, etc) and at its business premises, by a prominently displayed notice. For very large firms it may not be practical for every partner to be listed on the letterhead, and where there are more than 20 partners the requirement is satisfied by keeping at the firm's place of business a full list of partners, which must be available for inspection during office hours.

Unlawful partnerships

Individuals are essentially free to carry on their business or profession in their own way, so long as this does not threaten the public interest. Where individual freedom is likely to jeopardise the public interest, the law may intervene.

(1) RESTRICTIONS ON FREEDOM OF ASSOCIATION

(a) For most partnerships the general rule is that they must not consist of more than 20 people. Until recently, banking partnerships were limited to 10 people, but now they are no more restricted than other partnerships. Certain partnerships are, however, exempt from any restriction on numbers. At the moment exempt partnerships are solicitors, accountants, stockbrokers, patent agents, surveyors, estate agents, valuers, actuaries, consulting engineers, building designers, loss adjusters, insurance brokers and town planners.

(b) Certain professional rules act to restrain partnerships. For example:

- insurance business may not be conducted otherwise than by authorised persons (unless they are members of Lloyd's, a dispensation which may be removed before too long);
- under the Banking Act 1987, no banking business may be carried on by a firm without authorisation from the Bank of England;
- under the Consumer Credit Act 1974, every firm carrying on a consumer

credit business must acquire a licence from the Director General of Fair Trading;
– barristers may not form partnerships at all.

(c)   Under the Financial Services Act 1986, no one may carry on investment business in the United Kingdom without authority to do so. Those wishing to carry on such business must either seek authorisation from the Securities and Investment Board or, alternatively, join a recognised self-regulatory organisation, or obtain a certificate issued by a recognised professional body. Once authorisation has been obtained there must be continuing compliance with the detailed and complex regulatory framework laid down under the Financial Services Act 1986.

(d)   Many professional partnerships become unlawful if a partner ceases to hold a professional qualification. For example, a member of the Royal Institute of British Architects may not, without permission from the Institute, remain in partnership with someone who has been disqualified from membership of the Institute because of professional misconduct or for some other reason. Similarly, partnerships between registered and unregistered (or unqualified) dental practitioners are illegal and, indeed, it is considered to be professional misconduct for a dentist to enter into partnership with an unregistered person.

(2) COMPETITION

Free competition is part of our market philosophy. Article 85 of the Treaty of Rome, which set up the European Community, invalidates all agreements between businesses which may affect trade between member states of the Community if they seek to prevent, restrict or distort competition within the Common Market. There is also domestic legislation which sets out to control anti-competitive practices in the UK.

In both cases it is arguable that partnerships are inherently anti-competitive because everyone who enters into a partnership accepts, at least, an implied obligation not to compete with the firm's business (see Chapter 2). This point still has to be tested out fully before the British courts and the European Court of Justice.

(3) DISCRIMINATION

The Race Relations Act 1976 and the Sex Discrimination Act 1975 make it unlawful to discriminate against individuals on the grounds of race or sex. In particular, it is unlawful for any partnership, with more than six partners, to discriminate against a potential partner on the grounds of race or ethnic origin, or to expel a partner for similar reasons. The provision on sex discrimination is similar, except that it applies to a firm of any size.

(4) PUBLIC POLICY

A partnership may also be illegal for the more pervasive reason that it is formed for a purpose forbidden by the 'current notions of morality, religion or public policy'. The limits of such a broad concept may be a subject for debate, but it is clear that a partnership in the profits of crime (for example smuggling, theft or prostitution), would be illegal, as would a partnership formed for the making of profits out of a business which cannot be carried on except illegally (for example, an unlicensed bookmaking business). There is also some suggestion that a partnership may be illegal if it is in breach of 'international comity', which is a very elastic concept, but which could, perhaps, include a partnership set up to facilitate trading in breach of internationally imposed sanctions.

VARIATIONS ON A THEME: DIFFERENT TYPES OF PARTNERSHIP

National firms

In the professional arena the removal of the limitation on the size of many partnerships has permitted the growth of national firms of accountants in particular but also of chartered surveyors and, most recently, solicitors. Technically, a single partnership of several hundred partners is possible, but not very practical, and in these situations firms usually organise themselves into group partnerships, which are essentially partnerships between partnerships. Each local office will be a semi-autonomous partnership, but each will be linked by a partnership deed to a 'head' office, which is usually in London.

The precise structure of such a large organisation will be a matter for agreement. Questions, such as what the liability of a partner in one regional branch will be for the acts of the partners in another part of the country entirely, will be discussed and incorporated into the partnership agreement.

Companies as partners

As has been seen, it is quite possible for a limited company to be a partner in a firm and, indeed, there is nothing in the 1890 Act to prevent a partnership being composed entirely of companies. The use of companies as partners enables the size limits imposed upon partnerships to be overcome, since a company counts as one individual, however many members it may have. Companies also provide a means for a partnership to limit its liability, since, although a corporate partner is liable (without limit) for all the partnership debts, just as an individual would be, the partnership creditors, when pursuing their debts against a company, can only recover from that company's own resources and not from the resources of its shareholders.

International partnerships

There is no reason, in principle, why individuals from different legal jurisdictions should not all become partners under English law. Within the European Community, however, it has been difficult for partnerships to operate across frontiers because the national laws of the member states all have different versions of partnership.

Accordingly, to facilitate the creation of the single market, an entirely new form of supranational legal entity, called the European Economic Interest Grouping ('EEIG', and occasionally referred to as 'earwig'), has now emerged. The EEIG is designed for businesses which wish to co-operate at an international level, for example to pool resources for activities like research and development or marketing, or to engage in individual joint ventures. It is also envisaged that public bodies may wish to join forces through the medium of the EEIG to co-ordinate a joint approach to environmental problems, or to co-operate on cultural exchanges and tourism development programmes.

In the English sense, an EEIG is neither a partnership nor a company, but the rules which apply to it have an affinity with partnership law in that they are flexible and subject to contrary agreement between the parties involved.

Any business (whether a public or private company, partnership or sole trader) can join with others to set up an EEIG, provided that all are based in the EC and there are at least two members whose head offices or main activities are in different member states.

Unlike a partnership, an EEIG has a separate legal personality, so that it can engage in transactions with third parties. Like partnerships, however, the participating members have unlimited liability for the debts of the grouping, and any attempt to restrict that liability will be ineffective as far as the general public is concerned.

The main advantages of an EEIG are that it is easy and inexpensive to set up, flexible in structure, relatively free from red tape and fiscally transparent (profits and losses will be taxable only in the hands of members, as with a UK partnership). This avoids some of the complications of international tax laws. There are also disadvantages. In particular, an EEIG is intended to supplement rather than replace the economic activities of its members, which means that different businesses may not combine their main interests through this medium. In addition, the tax rules are full of uncertainties.

CHAPTER 2
Partners and Each Other

INTRODUCTION

A partnership, as a legal relationship, is based on two things:

(1) mutual trust and good faith, in that each partner is said to be in a fiduciary position vis-à-vis the other partners; and

(2) an agreement between the partners as to how their relationship will be conducted, which may be the result of initial negotiation and, therefore, specific, or which may be inferred from the partners' conduct when looked at with reference to the general law of partnership.

THE DUTY OF GOOD FAITH

The law presumes that partners will exhibit the utmost good faith in their dealings with one another. In other words, each partner must act honestly and honourably towards the other partners in the firm and must not allow his own interests to conflict with those of the firm. Technically, this duty is fundamental to a partnership in the sense that partners cannot agree not to be bound by it.

The duty manifests itself in three particular rules.

(1) Not to make unauthorised personal profit

If a partner makes a profit for himself from a transaction which ought properly to have been for the benefit of the partnership, he is in breach of his fiduciary duty and may be made to account to the partnership for the benefit he has received. So, for example, if a doctor, who practises in partnership with others, conducts insurance medicals outside normal surgery hours, he can be made to account for the fees to the partnership as a whole. The rule also extends to any use by a partner of the firm's property, name or business connection, and can apply even after the dissolution of the firm on the death of a partner (see p 79 below).

Technically, of course, a profit made by a partner from a transaction which is not related to the business at all is untouched by this rule, but the duty is strict and the partner is always likely to be put in the position of having to explain his conduct. Most problems tend to arise in situations where a partner makes a personal profit out of negotiating a deal on behalf of the partnership. However, the prohibition on benefiting from the firm's business connection is capable of casting the net much more broadly, and case law has recently thrown up some very difficult questions as to how far a partner may use 'partnership opportunities' in the form of information or contacts for a purpose which is not directly connected with the firm's business. The legal position is still far from certain and any partner wishing to use the business connection, for whatever reason, would be well-advised to consult his fellow partners before doing so. It should be emphasised here that a partner's liability to account for an unauthorised profit is not dependent upon the other partners having suffered a financial loss.

(2) To make full disclosure

It follows from what has been said already that partners must make full disclosure of all information relevant to the partnership. Again, the duty is strict and a simple failure to disclose, even without any fraudulent intention, will make a partner liable to the other partners for breach of duty. In particular, partners must render full and accurate accounts of any transactions affecting the partnership.

(3) Not to allow a conflict between duty and interest

A partner must not engage in any enterprise which is in competition with his firm, without accounting to the firm for all ensuing profits. Whether competition actually exists may be an interesting question in practice, and partners seeking to engage in outside activities would do well to take the other partners into their confidence. Usually, of course, breach of a partner's fiduciary duty will consist of both conflict of interest and unauthorised personal profit.

THE PARTNERSHIP AGREEMENT

The law does not require partnership agreements to be put into writing, but it is always sensible to do so as it may be difficult to prove the substance of an oral agreement if a dispute arises later on. Experience shows that partnership disputes can be just as traumatic as, and usually more complex than, divorce, and the importance of clear and precise drafting in partnership agreements cannot be over-estimated. Chapter 3 contains further discussion about partnership agreements and individual clauses which are commonly found in such agreements.

THE UNDERLYING LEGAL PRINCIPLES

If no written agreement exists, or, indeed, if an agreement exists but is incomplete, or has not been adhered to in practice, the ground rules on which that partnership is based will have to be inferred from the general law of partnership. The remainder of this chapter will deal with particular legal principles which are found, essentially, in the 1890 Act. However, it is important to bear in mind that the law fills gaps; in other words, any legal inference drawn in a given set of circumstances may always be superseded by a particular agreement between partners. The law is not prescriptive and this fact allows partnership to be a most flexible vehicle for carrying on a commercial or professional enterprise, subject only to the obvious point that good legal advice should be sought sooner rather than later.

Three particular topics need to be considered here:

(1) management and decision making;
(2) the financial structure of a partnership; and
(3) the enforcement of obligations between partners.

Chapter 8 (below) contains an extended discussion of partnership changes, which are another important aspect of internal relationships.

(1) Managing the partnership

The motto here is that he who bears the risks should have a say in how the enterprise is run. Except in the smallest of partnerships, however, this right is likely to be curtailed by the partnership agreement, since it may lead to ineffective management and, on occasion, to total paralysis of the firm. In the absence of agreement, the 1890 Act provides that each partner is entitled to participate in the management of the firm. More specifically, as regards decision making by the partnership, the 1890 Act goes on to draw a distinction between day-to-day matters, which are regarded as routine, and matters which go to the root of the partnership and are, consequently, regarded as fundamental. Routine decisions will be made by a majority of the partners. So, for example, the majority may properly decide that they wish to have a change in auditors or bankers, or that they wish to employ new staff. In the event of a split vote or a managerial stalemate a court, if asked to adjudicate, would always lean towards the status quo. In other words, there needs to be a positive vote for change.

The more 'fundamental' issues are changes in the nature of the partnership itself, for example the admission of a new partner, or the expulsion of an existing partner. In these circumstances, the unanimous consent of all partners is required, unless the partnership agreement expressly provides otherwise.

The distinction between day-to-day decisions and more fundamental issues is not without difficulty and, once again, the need to tighten up the general law by means of express provision in the partnership agreement should be emphasised.

RIGHT TO ACCOUNTS

Partnership accounts are dealt with in detail in Chapter 6. For these purposes, it is sufficient to state that every partner has a right to true accounts and to full information on all matters affecting the partnership. Additionally, the partnership books must be kept at the firm's place of business and must be open for inspection by the partners at any time.

RIGHT OF INDEMNITY

If a partner incurs a liability or makes a payment from his own pocket in respect of matters arising out of the ordinary and proper conduct of the partnership business, that partner has a right to be repaid such sum and protected ('indemnified') by the partnership against any liability which may arise. This right exists even if the expenditure proves to be unprofitable or commercially unwise.

Therefore, if a partner in, for example, a dental practice purchases a new autoclave to sterilise equipment, he is entitled to be re-imbursed from partnership funds or to be indemnified if any claim for non-payment is made against him.

The only situation in which the right of indemnity will not be available is if the partner in question is specifically restrained by the partnership agreement from incurring the particular liability or where he has acted fraudulently or negligently.

(2) The financial structure of a partnership

As has been seen (at Chapter 1) a partnership is a joint enterprise founded on the profit motive. Consequently, in financial terms there must be a sharing of profits and losses between partners, and the 1890 Act provides that, subject to contrary agreement, all partners are entitled to share equally in the capital and profits of the business and must contribute equally towards losses, whether of capital or otherwise. In practice such equal sharing is unusual, but it needs to be emphasised once again that, if the basic legal presumption is to be negatived, it must be expressly excluded by the partnership agreement (see Chapter 3).

PARTNERSHIP CAPITAL

All new partnerships need to fund the day-to-day running of the business before income starts to be generated. Whatever the nature of the business, staff salaries, office rental, business rates and other overheads will often have to be met before the work which such overheads represent can be converted into income. In addition, plant and equipment will probably need to be purchased before the business can get under way. In many professional firms, cash disbursements have to be made on behalf of clients and may not be recouped until later on.

Nowadays, most firms will finance their capital requirements by initial contributions in cash or kind from the partners. Subsequently, these contributions are likely to be re-inforced by borrowing and, as time goes on, by utilising undrawn profits. It is generally seen as equitable and, therefore, desirable, that partners should contribute capital in the profit-sharing ratio, so that those partners who enjoy a larger share of the firm's profits are also expected to risk a proportionately larger share of their capital. In some cases a partner's professional expertise may be considered so valuable that he will be credited with a share in the firm's capital without making a tangible contribution. In other cases, new, young partners may be permitted to build up their capital contributions over a number of years by way of deductions from their profit shares. It is worth noting, however, that such deductions will be made out of taxed income, so that it may be financially more attractive for a new partner to raise his capital contribution through a bank loan, on which the interest payments will attract tax relief.

The partnership agreement should always state the amounts paid, or credited as paid, by each partner and should set out the agreed capital-sharing ratio. In the absence of such provision, partners will be entitled to share capital equally if the firm is wound up, even though, as has been seen, their initial contributions are likely to have been unequal.

When a partner retires or leaves the partnership he is entitled to withdraw his capital from the firm. In many firms the senior partners will have contributed a disproportionate amount of capital and, as individual partners approach retirement, it will be important for these firms to take steps to address the problem. Repayments can sometimes be staggered over a period of time or, alternatively, junior partners may gradually increase their capital so as to allow the senior partners' shares to be reduced.

CAPITAL ACCOUNTS

The capital contributions should be shown separately in the partnership accounts. It is common accounting practice for undrawn profits to be credited to partners' capital accounts at the end of the financial year. It is undesirable, however, for partners to allow profits to be capitalised in this way without express agreement, as this can produce a huge imbalance in the capital shares and build up problems for later on. It is better accounting practice, therefore, for undrawn profits to be credited to the current account of each partner, and for the capital accounts to be confined strictly to the initial agreed capital contributions.

Drawings from a capital account are not permitted unless all partners consent. Once capital has been contributed a partner is not entitled to its return unless he ceases to be a partner. Equally, a partner cannot be compelled to increase his capital contribution without the agreement of all the partners. If the business is unsuccessful and the original capital has been exhausted, the partnership will have to be dissolved unless funds can be borrowed externally or the partners can agree to inject additional resources themselves.

INTEREST ON CAPITAL

Under the 1890 Act, a partner is explicitly not entitled to interest on his capital. In practice, it is quite usual to put a clause in the partnership agreement enabling interest on capital to be paid before the net profits are calculated and allocated. Such an arrangement can be used to counter-balance the common practice of crediting each partner with an annual 'salary' and allocating only the balance of the profits in the profit-sharing ratio.

Where, however, a partner makes an advance to the firm beyond the amount of capital which he originally agreed to put in, the 1890 Act provides that he is entitled to interest at the rate of five per cent on the advance. This provision should be modified or excluded by the partnership agreement, if only because the rate of interest specified is likely to be uneconomic.

CAPITAL PROFITS

Capital profits are profits which have arisen through an increase in the value of the partnership assets and, so, are conceptually separate from the profits of the business. If the firm is wound up such profits will be shared between the partners under their profit-sharing ratios and not on the basis of the original capital contributions. Accordingly, the partnership agreement should address this point if a different arrangement is required.

Finally, it must be emphasised that arrangements for the contribution and repayment of capital, whatever they may be, do not, in any way, affect an individual partner's unlimited liability for the debts of the firm.

DRAWINGS

Most partnerships will now accept the need for a clear policy on drawings. In theory, partners are entitled to an equal or otherwise prescribed share of the firm's annual profits. Since, however, these are only ascertained at the end of the financial year, there may be a real danger of partners drawing more money from the firm during the year than is justified by their final profit share. Even if this does not happen, an individual's drawings may still fluctuate over time, depending on his personal needs, and there may be an adverse effect on the cashflow position of the firm.

Accordingly, it will be normal for partners to agree on regular monthly drawings, which must allow for contingencies such as tax, and which must incur no risk of over-drawing. It may also be wise to prescribe a minimum drawings level in order to prevent older partners, whose family needs have diminished, from leaving too much money in the firm and so setting up problems later on.

PARTNERSHIP PROPERTY

Partnership property is any asset which is brought into, or acquired by, the firm and to which all partners are entitled.

In practice there is often some confusion over what property belongs to the firm and what property belongs to individual partners but which is used by the firm.

Why is the distinction important?

There are two main reasons.

(1) If property which belongs to the partnership increases in value, the partners will share the benefit. On the other hand, any increase in value in property belonging to an individual partner is his alone.

(2) If the firm is dissolved, partnership property will be available first to meet obligations to the firm's creditors. Only if there is a shortfall will partners' own property become available (for more details see Chapter 9).

Ideally, the partnership agreement (see Chapter 3) will determine the status of all assets which are used by the firm. Otherwise, the legal position under the 1890 Act will be that property which was part of the common pool when the business was established, or which was subsequently purchased with partnership funds, is presumed to belong to the partnership. Even property purchased by a partner out of his personal resources is susceptible to being viewed in the same light if it is treated and used as partnership property.

This does not mean, however, that assets used in connection with the firm's business will invariably be regarded as partnership property. Quite commonly, for instance, the land or premises from which the firm operates will be owned by an individual partner (see p 35). The tests will always be as follows.

(1) *What was the agreement, whether express or implied, between the partners regarding the ownership of the particular asset?*

Where there is a dispute the courts will not imply an agreement that property is to belong to the firm beyond what is absolutely necessary to give business efficacy to the relationship between the partners. Once again, therefore, the need to deal with ownership of property through the partnership agreement must be emphasised.

(2) *If there is no agreement, what would be a reasonable inference to draw as regards ownership?*

For example, if the firm is paying rent to an individual partner in respect of the partnership premises, it may be natural to assume that ownership of the premises remains in the individual partner, and that they have not become partnership property.

Further discussion of some of the legal technicalities relating to partnership property, particularly land, can be found in Chapter 4.

PARTNERSHIP SHARES

The basic principle in relation to partnership shares is that partners benefit equally from partnership profits and contribute equally to partnership losses. In many partnerships, however, this will not be a satisfactory arrangement, and the partnership agreement will lay down different rules.

The term 'share' is often used in relation to a partner's entitlement to the assets of the firm, including profits. Legally speaking, a partner's share comprises the proportion of partnership assets to which he is entitled after those assets have been realised and converted into money, and after payment of all partnership debts and liabilities. Unless otherwise agreed, partnership shares will be equal.

While the firm is a going concern, a partnership share is, essentially, a future interest in a pool of assets, and each partner is entitled to require those assets to be applied only for the purposes of the firm. Realisation of assets takes place when the partnership comes to an end, which occurs either because of the departure of an individual partner or by a general dissolution of the firm. At this point, all partners' interests 'crystallise' and they are entitled to insist on the assets being applied, first, towards payment of the firm's debts and, secondly, divided amongst the partners in the appropriate proportions. As will be seen (see Chapter 8), although the 1890 Act states that a partnership must be dissolved when a partner dies, retires or is expelled, in practice the partnership agreement will provide for the relationship to continue, notwithstanding such a change. In these circumstances, it will clearly be inappropriate for all the partnership assets to be converted into cash and distributed, and the partnership agreement should consequently formulate how an outgoing partner's share will be valued and paid out.

THE PARTNER'S LIEN

The partner's lien describes the right of a partner to insist that partnership property is eventually applied in payment of partnership debts and then divided amongst the partners. Its significance is that it may operate to prevent the disposal of partnership assets (although not so as to prevent normal business), and it extends to debts owed by partners to the firm. Therefore, where a partner owes money to the firm and also to other creditors, the firm's debt will be protected. The lien also affects the executors of a partner who has died or the trustee in bankruptcy of an insolvent partner. (Insolvency is considered more generally in Chapter 9.)

THE TRANSFER OF A PARTNERSHIP SHARE

Partnership is very much a personal relationship and it is quite reasonable, therefore, that partners should not be called on to accept a partner substitute if one partner wishes to sell his partnership share to someone else. The law confirms this in the principle that no person can be introduced as a partner without the consent of all other members of the firm.

This does not mean, however, that a partner cannot dispose of his financial interest in the firm. For example, when a partner dies, his estate will benefit from his share in the partnership assets. His executors or relatives will, however, have no right to insist on being admitted to the partnership itself and, consequently, at this point the financial interest in the partnership becomes separated from the normal power of a partner to manage and control the firm. Again, if a partner seeks to make a life-time transfer of his share, the financial benefit will be passed on, but the transferee will not be permitted to stand in the shoes of the partner vis-à-vis the firm or to interfere in any way in the affairs of the firm, unless this is acceptable to all the partners.

SHARES IN A LIMITED COMPANY

It is important not to confuse a partnership share with a share in a limited company. The liability of a partner in a firm is unlimited, so that his partnership share is available to satisfy creditors of the firm. That personal liability remains in him so long as he remains a partner, irrespective of whether he decides to transfer his financial interest in the firm to someone else.

A shareholder in a limited company, on the other hand, has no liability to the company beyond the duty to pay for his shares. As a general rule, company shares may be bought and sold like any other piece of property. Once a shareholder sells his shares, his name is removed from the company's register and his interest in the company ceases.

(3) Enforcement of mutual obligations ★★★

Partnerships are based on agreements which may be specifically drafted (the ideal situation), *or* inferences may be drawn from the way a partnership is conducted, *or*, in the final analysis, the provisions of the 1890 Act will be read into the relationship and will become, in effect, the terms of a hypothetical agreement. Any agreement or contract, formal or not, will create mutual rights and duties. Therefore, any partner may enforce his rights against the others and, in turn, is susceptible to having enforcement proceedings brought against him. Because a firm has no independent legal status (see Chapter 1, above) a partner who sues the firm is technically suing himself along with the other partners and this used to be a bar to inter-partner litigation. Now, however, partners may sue, or be sued, in the name of the firm.

CHAPTER 3
The Partnership Agreement ★★★

'In every age and clime we see,
Two of a trade can ne'er agree.' (John Gay)

INTRODUCTION

That intending partners should seriously consider entering into a formal partnership agreement has been, and will be, emphasised throughout this book. 'Gentleman's agreements' have a habit of facilitating prize fights, and goodwill and co-operation between highly qualified and normally highly civilised individuals can vanish overnight. Only too frequently, partners fail to appreciate, until they are on the threshold of a major dispute, that they do not have any internal rules which are capable of producing a satisfactory outcome. Where there is no partnership agreement, or the agreement is not sufficiently comprehensive, the provisions of the Partnership Act 1890 ('the 1890 Act') and the general rules developed through case law will be applied to the situation, and may produce radically different consequences than the partners would have wished. At that stage, the thought that such consequences could have been anticipated and averted by preparation of an appropriate partnership agreement, is likely to be extremely galling.

It seems that professional partners are particularly prone to ignore the need for a partnership agreement until it is too late – indeed, firms of solicitors quite frequently come into this category! The moral of this is that professional qualifications and high, professional standards do not prevent problems from arising in a working relationship, and where both commercial and professional considerations have to be taken into account the relationship between partners is likely to be more complex and, consequently, more volatile than in a straightforward partnership.

DRAFTING THE PARTNERSHIP AGREEMENT ★★★

The preparation of a partnership agreement is a skilled job and legal advice should always be sought. Good draftsmanship will produce a document which is comprehensive, precise, in plain English, and which covers every foreseeable problem which could arise in a partnership relationship. It should not be necessary to seek legal advice, whenever a problem crops up, if the basic agreement meets the above criteria. Consequently, the initial legal fees should be money very well spent.

In order to be fully comprehensive the partnership agreement should deal with the areas of the relationship covered by the 1890 Act, as well as areas which are not so covered. This is because the provisions in the 1890 Act will be deemed to apply to any partnership unless the partners agree that they should not. Whilst implied agreements are common, as has been explained already (see p 13), it is much more satisfactory if all the ground rules are contained in one document, and the 1890 Act is expressly excluded where it is not intended that it should apply.

CHECKLIST FOR PREPARING PROFESSIONAL PARTNERSHIP AGREEMENTS

Not every partnership will wish to cover every aspect of the relationship in its partnership agreement. The exent to which it does so will depend upon the amount of certainty it seeks.

Partners should review the adequacy of their partnership agreement from time to time. In doing so, they may find the following provides a useful checklist.

(1) Who is to join in the agreement?

- Who are to be the partners?

- Do all the partners or proposed partners have the necessary professional qualifications (see p 8)?

- How many partners will there be? Are they permitted to practise in partnerships of more than 20 (see p 7)?

- How will additional partners be admitted to the firm? (For instance, will the unanimous consent of all existing partners be required, or will a majority be sufficient?)

- Does the firm recognise salaried partners? On what terms? Should they be parties to the agreement (see p 93)?
- Will any partners enjoy a special status, eg senior partners, a managing partner?
- If the firm consists of more than six partners, will any provision regarding membership of the firm be discriminatory on the grounds of race (see p 8)?
- Will any provision be discriminatory on grounds of sex (see p 8)?

(2) The firm's business

- What will the firm's business be?
- Will the firm be carrying on investment business? If so, are the partners members of a recognised professional body? If not, are the partners members of a recognised self-regulating organisation (see p 8)?
- What professional requirements must be observed in the conduct of investment business and how should the agreement take account of these?

(3) Commencement of business

- Is the firm already in existence (see Chapter 1)?
- What is the intended commencement date?
- Is it possible that the enterprise will have been embarked on before the chosen date (see p 5)?

(4) Duration

- Is the partnership intended to be for a fixed term?
- What events will cause the partnership to terminate?
- What events are *not* intended to bring about a termination (for example, death, retirement, expulsion, bankruptcy, or a partner ceasing to hold a necessary qualification (see, generally, Chapter 8)?
- Will termination be permitted at the instigation of any one individual?
- Will the partners be able to extend the duration of the partnership? If so, how?

(5) Firm name

- Has the firm complied with the Business Names Act 1985 (see p 6)?

- Is the firm's stationery correct? Does the firm's name incorporate any impermissible words (for example, the name of a firm of solicitors may only consist of the names of one or more of the principals)?

(6) Place(s) of business

- Where will the firm carry on business?

- Will the business premises become an asset of the firm?

- If the premises will continue to belong to a partner, on what terms will the firm occupy them (for example, by a lease, a formal licence, an informal licence)?

- Will the property-owning partner receive any rent or other payment in respect of the firm's occupation? If so, how will the money be paid?

- Is it intended that additional premises/branch offices be opened? If so, how will the decision be taken? How will each branch office be managed? How will profits be dealt with?

- Will the lease or freehold interest in the premises be vested in trustee partners? How will trustees be replaced?

(7) Capital

- How much capital is to be put into the firm?

- How is capital to be contributed?

- Will partners own the capital pro-rata, according to their contributions?

- Will interest on capital be paid? At what rate?

- Will there be provision for additional capital contributions?

- Will the capital structure be alterable? How will this be determined?

- Will there be provision for partners to make loans to the firm? What will be the terms?

(8) Partnership assets

- What will partnership assets be?

- Who owns what? (It will be helpful to prepare a list of intended partnership assets.)

- Does goodwill have any value as between partners? (Most professional partnership agreements will provide that goodwill is to be regarded as having no value as far as transactions between partners are concerned.)
- Will an outgoing partner receive the value of his share of the goodwill? If so, how will this be valued?
- Will goodwill be shown as an asset in the firm's balance sheet? (This would be most unusual in professional partnerships.)

(9) Profits and losses

- Will profits and losses be shared equally between partners, or in some other ratio?
- Will income, profits and losses be shared differently from capital profits and losses?
- Will any partner receive a 'salary' out of profits before the balance is shared?
- How will the partners' shares be expressed (for example, as a percentage, fraction, or in terms of income points)?
- Will any deduction be made for illness or incapacity of a partner, or for maternity leave?
- Will there be preferential shares?
- Will there be incentive shares?
- What will be the drawings policy (for example, will there be fixed monthly drawings)? If so, who will decide on the level of drawings?
- Will overdrawing be permitted? If so, on what terms?
- How will tax provision be made?
- How will the shares of new partners be determined?
- How (if at all) will it be possible to vary a partner's existing share of profits or losses?

(10) Provision for existing debts or fees

- Are there any existing debts or liabilities? (It would be helpful to prepare a list of these. This question will be particularly relevant where a new partnership agreement is being prepared for an existing firm, perhaps on the admission of a new partner.)
- How will existing debts/fees be shared between the partners?

(11) Bankers

[Note that client accounts have to be maintained by solicitors, accountants, architects and firms carrying on investment business under the Financial Services Act 1986.]

- Who will be the firm's bankers?
- Who will have authority to sign cheques?
- How many signatures will be needed?
- Will cheques above a certain level require additional signatures?
- What different types of account will be needed?

(12) Books

- Where will the firm's books be kept?
- Are the partners obliged to make entries (for example, where the firm carries on investment business under the Financial Services Act 1986)?
- Will all partners have access to the books?
- Will salaried partners have access to the books?
- Will separate capital accounts be maintained in the books?

(13) Annual accounts

- What will the accounting date be?
- Who will be the firm's accountants?
- How may the accountants be changed?
- Is goodwill to be shown in the accounts?
- How is work in progress to be shown in the accounts, and at what value?
- Will the accounts be audited?
- By whom will the accounts be signed?
- Will there be any provision for interim accounts?

(14) Duties of partners

- Will all partners be required to devote their time and attention exclusively to the practice?

- Will partners be permitted to involve themselves in other activities (for example, taking on directorships, taking on consultancies, lecturing engagements)?

- How will fees from partners' outside activities be dealt with?

- Should there be a reference in the agreement to the partners' duty of good faith? (This will be implied in any event (see p 11) but an express reference will be helpful to remind the partners of their obligations in this respect.)

(15) Restrictions on the authority of partners

- What will be the nature of any restriction on the authority of partners (for example, will it be confined to junior partners)?

- What will be the scope of any restriction on authority (for example, as to taking trainees, hiring/firing, dealing with particular clients, incurring particular liabilities)?

(16) Decision-making

- What will be the procedure for decision-making (for example, provision for meetings, notice, size of quorum, attendance of non-voting partners, proxies, casting votes, rights of veto)?

- Which partnership decisions will require unanimous approval?

- Which decisions can be made by a majority?

- What will be the required size of any majority?

- Who will have voting rights (for example, as to lending money, giving guarantees, disposing of partnership assets)?

(17) Holidays or other leave

- What will be the permitted length of holidays?

- Will there be a maximum/minimum holiday entitlement or requirement?

- Can holidays be carried forward?

- What will be the priority between partners?

- How much holiday can be taken at one time?

- Will there be any entitlement to sabbatical leave?

- Will there be any entitlement to maternity leave?

- Will there be any entitlement to paternity leave?
- If any special leave is to be taken, what will be the period of notice? What will be the financial entitlement?

(18) Health of partners

- Does any partner's health require special consideration?
- Will partners be obliged to effect health insurance?
- Will partners be required to have regular medical examinations?
- Will the results of medicals be disclosed to other partners?

(19) Cars

- Will a car be provided for each partner?
- What will be the range of choice?
- What will be the value?
- How often will cars be replaced?
- Who will own cars where partners make a personal contribution to the purchase price?
- Who will be responsible for maintenance costs?
- What provisions should be made to cover fuel costs?

(20) Insurance

- Is professional indemnity insurance necessary? Is it a condition of practice?
- Should consideration be given to insuring against professional negligence and public liability? (Note that it is essential to insure against employers' compulsory liability.)
- Will there be any provision regarding insurance of partnership assets? (This would be unusual.)
- Will partners be required to effect other insurance (for example, life assurance, retirement annuity contracts or personal pension arrangements, health insurance)?
- Should term assurance to buy out a retiring partner be considered?
- Should loss of profits insurance be considered?
- How will premiums be paid?

(21) **Retirement**

- How much notice must a partner give of impending retirement?
- Will there be any post-retirement consultancy arrangements?
- Will there be a provision for a compulsory retirement age? If so, will this requirement discriminate against female partners?
- Will partners be required to retire after prolonged incapacity through physical or mental illness?
- Will it be possible to give compulsory notice of retirement? Will all remaining partners have to agree?

(22) **Expulsion**

- What will be the grounds for expulsion of a partner (for example, serious breaches of the partnership agreement, failure to account for money, bankruptcy, conduct likely to harm the business)? (Note that these grounds must not breach anti-discrimination legislation.)
- What will be the manner of decision-making regarding expulsion?
- Will the unanimous consent of all partners be needed?
- Will the partner facing expulsion be given an opportunity to be heard?
- Will there be provision for suspension pending expulsion?
- Will there be an arbitration procedure if an expulsion is disputed?

(23) **Consequences of death, retirement or expulsion**

- Will continuing partners be bound to acquire an outgoing partner's share? Will they have an option to do so? (Note the importance of business property relief for inheritance tax.)
- If partners have an option, on what terms will it be exercisable? How will the money be raised?
- What will be the outgoing partner's entitlement ('share') (for example with regard to return of capital, undrawn profits to date, accrued interest on capital account, surplus assets, work in progress, goodwill)?
- What will be the valuation process?
- How will repayment of advances be dealt with?
- Will payments out be made by instalments?

- Will there be provision for retentions (for example, to cover tax or other potential liabilities)?

- Will an annuity be payable to an outgoing partner or to the dependants of a partner who has died?

- What will be the procedure for divesting and re-vesting the legal title to the business premises (see Chapter 4)?

- Will continuing partners take over all the existing debts of the firm?

- How and by whom will notification of the partner's departure be given?

- What books must be delivered up?

- Will the outgoing partner subsequently have a right to inspect the books?

- Will the outgoing partner be obliged to make a continuation election for tax purposes (see p 66) and will the continuing partners indemnify him against any personal loss?

- Will there be any restraint on competition by an outgoing partner?

- Should any restraint on competition be against: soliciting clients or patients of the firm; acting for clients of the firm; practising within a certain area; or practising in a particular field?

- What will be the time-limit for any restraint on competition?

- Will any such restraint be seen as an unreasonable restraint on trade, or does it contravene Article 85 of the Treaty of Rome?

(24) Admission of new partners

- How will the decision to admit new partners be taken?

- At what date will a new partner become liable as such?

- What will be the new partner's capital contribution?

- How will it be paid?

- When will it be paid?

- What adjustments will have to be made to existing capital accounts?

- Will a new partner be required to join in making a continuation election for tax purposes, and will he be indemnified against any individual loss?

(25) **Dissolution/winding up**

- When may the partnership be dissolved?
- What will be the procedure for dissolution?
- Will partners have the right to purchase partnership assets on a winding up?
- Is any partner to have special authority during a winding up?
- Is any partner's authority to be restricted during a winding up?

(26) **Arbitration or alternative dispute resolution**

- Will arbitration or alternative dispute resolution be preferred to resorting to court?
- Who will appoint an arbitrator/mediator?
- What will be the extent of the arbitrator's powers?
- Who will recommend an appropriate alternative dispute resolution procedure?
- If alternative dispute resolution is unsuccessful will the dispute be referred to arbitration?

(27) **Notices**

- What will be the ways and means of serving notices relating to partnership matters?

(28) **Amendments to the partnership agreement**

- How will amendments to the partnership agreement be carried out?
- How will amendments be recorded?

(29) **Costs**

- How will the costs of preparing the partnership agreement be borne?

CHAPTER 4
Partnership Property

INTRODUCTION

In Chapter 2 we noted the importance of making a clear distinction between property which is regarded as belonging to the firm and property which continues to be owned by an individual partner, albeit used in the firm's business.

The essential legal point is that it is up to the partners themselves to agree what assets are to be treated as partnership property and only in the absence of agreement will the law intervene. It is wise to specify, in the partnership agreement, property which belongs to the firm and property which remains in the ownership of individual partners.

OWNERSHIP

The legal principles which will apply in the absence of agreement are as follows.

(1) Property paid for by the firm belongs to the firm. Therefore, if office equipment is bought with partnership money, that equipment will be partnership property.

(2) Property acquired by a partner for the benefit of the firm, **and** which is used and treated as partnership property, will belong to the firm, even if the individual partner actually paid for it. Use of an asset alone, particularly where the asset is land, does not make it partnership property.

(3) Secret profits obtained by a partner in breach of his duty of good faith (see p 11) will be treated as belonging to the partnership.

(4) Goodwill constitutes partnership property.

(5) Assets brought into the firm by way of a partner's capital contribution become partnership property.

(6) Partners may, at any time, agree to introduce assets to or remove assets from the common pool. Creditors of the firm have no right to prevent property from being taken out of the firm as long as there is no fraudulent intention, and as long as the firm is not insolvent.

Some technical and practical points

It is worth noting that the law attaches one or two arcane technicalities to the ownership of partnership property. Legal advice will, of course, be necessary if a firm acquires premises or land in which to carry on a profession or business. However, because other partnership property or equipment will be subject to many of the same technicalities, a brief explanation will be given here.

'UNDIVIDED SHARES'

All partnership property is held by partners in 'undivided shares'. That means that each partner has an unliquidated but quantifiable share of the entire property which he can sell, mortgage or leave by will to someone else. So, for example, if A, B and C are in partnership, and the firm owns office premises, A will be able to bequeath his interest in this property to his widow on his death.

Legally, this is a special arrangement which is applied to partners because they have a commercial relationship. As between spouses, on the other hand, the position may be different. Spouses are likely to enjoy a joint interest in the matrimonial home, which will pass automatically to the survivor on the death of one of them, but which cannot be the subject of a disposition by will. This alternative type of co-ownership is known as 'joint tenancy', and will never apply to partnership property.

'CONVERSION'

English law recognises two broad categories of property: real property and personal property. Real property is land, and rights over land which have a value, for example rights of way over someone else's land. Personal property is more or less everything else, for example money, shares, equipment, collectables, cars, intangible assets like debts or copyright, and so on. Buildings, machinery or plant, which are attached to land, become legally part of the land, and so are real property rather than personal property.

Nowadays there is no real significance in the distinction between real and personal property. In the past, whether property was considered to be real property or personal property may have determined to whom it passed if the owner died without leaving a will. Where partnership property is concerned the position is curious, because the law treats *all* partnership property, including land and buildings, as personal property and not real property. This means that a partner's share of the partnership assets, whatever they may be, will be regarded as personal property. The only significance today is that this may affect a partner's tax position on death.

'LAND AS PARTNERSHIP PROPERTY' ★★★

Land (or buildings) owned by a firm can be vested in no more than four partners and no fewer than two. This means that four (or fewer) partners' names will appear in the legal documentation, and they alone will be able to transfer ownership of the land to a third party (for example on a change of business premises). These named partners are trustees for themselves and for all the other partners; technically, therefore, if the land is sold they will receive the proceeds of sale and will then have to account to the partnership for them. Trustee partners should be replaced as they retire or die; if only one partner remains the land cannot be dealt with until a further appointment is made.

Sometimes, partnership premises may not be owned outright, but may be rented or leased. This means that the firm will pay rent in return for the exclusive occupation of the premises for an agreed period of time.

Where a firm is proposing to take on a lease, strictly speaking only the trustee partners need to be made the official signatories. Some landlords, however, may insist that all partners join in, either as actual parties or as sureties, to underwrite the obligations taken on by the trustee partners.

'BUSINESS LEASES' ★★★

Security of tenure
Where the firm's premises are leased the normal security of occupation available to all business tenants will be extended to partners. The Landlord and Tenant Act 1954 allows a business tenant to claim renewal of a lease which has come to an end unless the landlord has a valid objection, prescribed by the Act. This right is available even where the membership of the firm is different at the time of claiming a renewal from that at the grant of the lease, perhaps because partners have retired, or new partners have been admitted to the firm. Similar rules apply to farming partnerships under the Agricultural Holdings Act 1986.

The 1954 Act imposes stringent procedures for claiming renewal and legal advice should always be taken, preferably well before a lease comes to an end. More generally, the negotiation and drafting of business leases takes considerable professional expertise; provisions for rent review, in particular, can be a minefield for the inexperienced.

If, as sometimes happens, the firm's premises are owned by one of the partners but leased to the firm as a whole, there may be a potential conflict where the firm applies for a renewal of the tenancy under the security provisions. The landlord/partner, wearing his landlord's hat, will need to approve the renewal, and the question then will be: must he act for the benefit of the partnership as a whole, or may he pursue his own individual interest as landlord? The legal position here is rather unclear. In essence, the answer will depend upon whether the court thinks that his activities are within the scope of his fiduciary obligations as partner (see Chapter 2). It is not legally possible for partners, as co-owners of premises, to grant a lease to themselves.

Transferability

An interest under a lease, like any other piece of property, is transferable. Most professionally drawn leases seek to impose restrictions or prohibitions on transfer so that landlords do not find themselves inadvertently saddled with unsuitable tenants. This may raise technical problems for a firm where there is a change of partners and the lease needs to be transferred from the old firm to the new. In general, the consent of the landlord will have to be obtained and a firm should always seek to ensure that its landlord is prevented from objecting to such a formal transfer. The partnership agreement should always require an outgoing partner to execute a transfer of the lease where this is necessary, and there should be a corresponding requirement to replace an outgoing partner as lessee.

'GOODWILL'

Goodwill is the difference between the value of a business as a going concern and the value of its assets, or, more specifically, the advantages of the reputation and connection of the firm. All businesses generate goodwill to some extent, and in a professional partnership the goodwill may be substantial. In a partnership, goodwill is usually a partnership asset, although it is unusual to show it as such in the balance sheet, mainly because that can be very misleading.

Disputes about goodwill tend to arise where a firm splits up, where partners die or retire, or where a new partner is introduced.

In most professions goodwill is saleable, although nowadays it is less common to require a new partner to buy himself into the firm. In the medical profession, however, the National Health Service Act 1977 makes it illegal to sell the goodwill of an NHS general practice. This restriction does not affect the sale of the goodwill in a wholly private practice.

Protecting goodwill and restraining competition   ★★★

When a partner leaves the firm, for whatever reason, the remaining partners will naturally wish to protect their goodwill by restraining the outgoing partner from entering into competition with them. Where, as is usual, the remaining partners purchase the outgoing partner's share of the goodwill, they will be doubly concerned to restrain his subsequent activities.

The law says that it is permissible to impose restraints on the activities of an outgoing partner as long as they do not unreasonably restrict his freedom to practise his own profession. Courts will generally be less tough on restraints between partners than on restraints between employer and employee, because in the former the goodwill is likely to have been transferred to the remaining partners when a partner leaves a firm, and they are entitled to protect that.

Otherwise, it seems that what is reasonable will depend largely upon the nature of the firm and its practice, and the position of the former partner within the firm. Restraint clauses should be included in the partnership agreement, but very careful drafting is needed, because if a clause is considered unreasonable it will be struck out entirely, rather than modified, by the court. Consequently, by seeking to over-restrain an outgoing partner, those partners left in the firm may end up wholly unprotected.

There has been a good deal of litigation concerning restraint clauses in medical partnerships. It used to be accepted that a private practice could be protected by a restraint clause, but that no such restraint could be taken in relation to a NHS practice. It was argued that it would be contrary to public policy to do so since it would prevent a doctor from complying with his public obligations to care for patients and that, as it is unlawful to sell the goodwill in a NHS practice, there is nothing valuable which partners can justifiably seek to protect by a restraint clause. In 1987, however, the Court of Appeal rejected these arguments, and held that no distinction now needs to be drawn between restraints imposed in respect of a firm engaged in private practice, and restraints affecting a firm practising wholly or partly within the NHS. Having said that, there is still no guarantee that an outgoing partner's list of patients will automatically be taken over by his remaining partners, because NHS lists are restricted in size, and because the Family Health Services Authority has ultimate control over the lists.

Interestingly, restraints affecting NHS dental practices do not give rise to the same difficulties, because dental lists are not restricted or formalised in the way that medical lists are. Clearly, therefore, goodwill in a NHS dental practice is freely saleable, and is likely to be of greater value than goodwill in a NHS medical practice.

CHAPTER 5

Partners and the Outside World

'All for One and One for All'
Dumas, *The Three Musketeers*

LIABILITY OF PARTNERS IN BUSINESS TRANSACTIONS

In business transactions any individual, including a partner, will be personally liable for the debts or other obligations which he incurs, and may ultimately be sued on them. In addition, a partner is responsible, without limit, for debts and obligations incurred by any of his partners whilst acting on behalf of the partnership, and a firm is responsible, without limit, for the debts and other liabilities incurred by any of the partners. So, for example, if A, B and C are in partnership, and B orders some equipment from X Limited, which is duly delivered, X Limited will be able to recover the purchase price from A or B or C, or from the firm ABC, which may be sued in the firm's name.

This principle is limited only by the rule that a partner must have authority to engage in business transactions on behalf of the firm.

A partner's authority can arise in two ways:

(1) he may have *express* or *actual* authority, specifically given to him by his partners; or

(2) he may have *implied* or *ostensible* authority, which will stem from the presumption that someone in his position is authorised to carry out a particular transaction.

It has been emphasised up to now that internal relations within a firm are a matter for agreement between partners, and that partners are well advised to legislate for themselves in that area. Here, however, the position is different, in that the legal position of the firm, vis-à-vis the outside world, is regulated by the general law in the Partnership Act 1890 ('the 1890 Act'), and not by the partnership agreement. Therefore, even if the agreement purports to limit the authority of individual partners to carry out transactions on behalf of the firm, any such limitation will not necessarily affect the outside world. As we shall see, an outsider will often be able to take a partner's authority for granted, whatever the firm's internal rules may be.

At this point it is worth comparing the legal position of a limited company. The limited company, as a legal person, will engage in legal transactions and the company alone will be liable for the consequences. Whilst the directors may be the eyes and ears of a company, they are not responsible for its debts and the same applies to shareholders once their shares are fully paid up. That is what is meant by 'limited liability'.

(1) **Actual authority**

A partner may be given actual authority either by the terms of the partnership agreement itself, or by a one-off agreement with the other partners.

Therefore, if a partner in a firm of chartered surveyors is given authority to purchase photographic equipment, the firm will be bound to pay for it. Similarly, if an architect in partnership is authorised to enter into contracts with a local authority for provision of professional services, the firm is bound to honour them.

From an outsider's point of view, actual authority is most important when the outsider transacts with a partner in circumstances which appear to be outside the firm's usual range of business. As we shall see, in 'normal' transactions, a partner's *ostensible* authority is what really determines the liability of his co-partners for his activities. But, in the one-off situation, the outsider will need to rely on actual authority and should protect his position by checking whether or not actual authority exists.

(2) **Ostensible or apparent authority**

In practice ostensible or apparent authority is most important. The principle is that if a partner appears to have authority to engage in a particular kind of business activity, an outsider to the firm should be able to rely on appearances. In these circumstances, whether or not a partner has actual authority may be immaterial.

The 1890 Act states that a partner who acts in the usual course of the firm's business will have ostensible authority, and, therefore, will bind the firm unless the person with whom he is dealing knows that he has no authority or does not know that he is a partner.

The key questions here can be shown in terms of a flow chart.

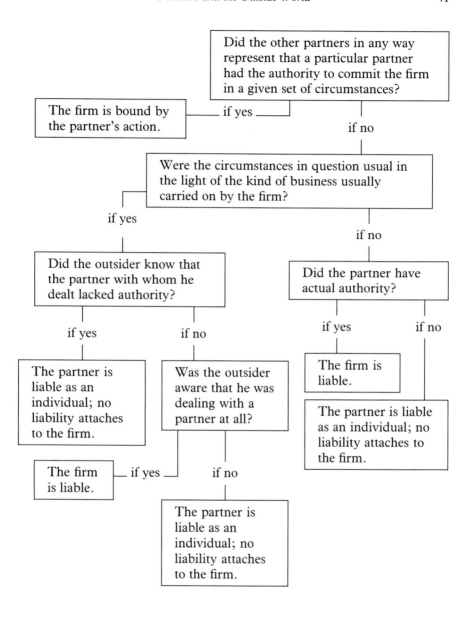

Fig 1   *Outsiders dealing with partners: key questions*

THE CONTENT OF OSTENSIBLE AUTHORITY

It is useful to have in mind particular powers which are covered by a partner's ostensible authority. Clearly, however, the ostensible authority for different types of business or professional partnerships may vary, and if the existence of such authority ever became an issue in court, expert evidence of fact might be needed.

It is also important to notice that what is 'usual', even in a particular business, may change over time. For example, the Financial Services Act 1986 has clearly affected the understanding of 'usual' business for the different categories of professionals working in the financial advice field.

Examples of powers within the ostensible authority of *all* partners would be:

(1) buying and selling goods used in or produced by the business;
(2) incurring other trade debts;
(3) drawing a cheque in the firm's name or stopping payment on a cheque;
(4) accepting payment of debts and giving valid receipts;
(5) hiring and firing employees of the firm;
(6) insuring the firm's property;
(7) bringing or defending legal proceedings.

Examples of powers which would not be within the ostensible authority of partners would be:

(1) taking a lease on behalf of the firm;
(2) mortgaging partnership land;
(3) giving guarantees on behalf of the firm.

In addition, there is one major difference between the ostensible authority of trading partners, and that of non-trading partners (partners in firms of accountants, architects, auctioneers, quantity surveyors, doctors, and dentists and the like), in that the latter may not have ostensible authority to borrow money on behalf of the firm. The case law on this point is now dated, and out of touch with the fact that nowadays many professional partnerships are financed by borrowed money, but it is still unsafe for an architect or a dentist, for example, who is practising in partnership, to overdraw on the firm's account without the agreement of his partners, because he may find that he alone is subsequently liable to the bank.

(3) Other sources of liability

Firms may become liable in two further situations for business transactions in which individuals engage.

(1) RATIFICATION

Partners can always ratify a business arrangement made by one of them without actual or ostensible authority. That means that the arrangement will become binding on the partners when, following normal principles, it would not.

(2) HOLDING OUT

A person holds himself out to be a partner if, by what he says or writes, or by his conduct, he invites others to draw the conclusion that he is a partner. Following on from the rules already outlined in this chapter, it will be clear that in these circumstances he will be liable as a partner for the actions of his fellow partners, on the principle that the law will not allow him to deny the fact that he has encouraged others to believe that he is a partner.

For example, if the name of a former partner continues to appear on a firm's headed notepaper, an outsider will be entitled to regard that individual as still being a partner, unless he has notice to the contrary. Similarly, when a partner retires it is essential to give notice to all the customers or clients of the firm; otherwise the retiring partner will remain liable for partnership debts incurred after the date of his retirement. It is also important that consultants or others who do work for or on behalf of a partnership should ensure that the nature of their relationship with the firm is clearly set out in all correspondence with outsiders.

NEW PARTNERS

A person who is admitted as a partner into an existing firm does not, as a rule, become liable for anything done before he became a partner.

OUTGOING PARTNERS

By contrast, a partner who leaves or retires from a firm remains liable for obligations incurred before his retirement, but is not generally liable for those incurred after that date. The exception is where an outsider deals with the firm whilst under the impression that the outgoing partner is still a member of the firm; this emphasises the importance of giving notice of major partnership changes. For established clients or customers, it is usual to send out individual notices of partnership changes. By themselves, however, these notices are not sufficient protection for an outgoing partner because they will not cover customers or clients new to the firm, who are aware of his connection with the firm and not of his departure. To cover this situation the partners should publish a notice in the *London Gazette*, which is the official channel for communicating information of this sort to the outside world.

WRONGFUL ACTS COMMITTED BY PARTNERS

Wrongful acts committed by partners can be either criminal acts or, more usually, acts which cause loss or injury to others through a partner's negligence. Criminal acts have to be prosecuted by the State, and there may be a range of penalties depending on the severity of the offence, most commonly fines or imprisonment. Other wrongful acts are private matters, which the victim, or (more usually these days) his insurers, will pursue through the civil courts against the wrongdoer, and liability will result in the payment of financial compensation to the injured party. Civil, as opposed to criminal, wrongs are known as torts.

Torts

Any individual, who happens to be a partner, will carry personal liability for his own wrongful acts. Beyond that, the 1890 Act makes the firm liable for the torts of a partner acting in the ordinary course of the business of the firm or with the authority of his co-partners. Torts include deliberate acts, such as assault or defamation. However, nowadays, negligence is by far the greatest potential source of liability.

The principle on which liability rests is in fact very similar to that which determines the liability of an employer for the wrongful acts of his employee. The main problem is how to define 'ordinary course of business' since it is perfectly arguable that it is never in the ordinary course of a firm's business to commit a wrongful act. The real test here is – was the partner who committed the tort engaged in ordinary partnership business at the time, even though what he did was clearly not what he was authorised to do? For example, if an accountant negligently conducts an audit he will be acting in the course of his firm's business, which clearly involves non-negligent auditing.

Similarly, where a partner injures a pedestrian by driving negligently on his way to a meeting with clients the firm will be liable because he was engaged in the ordinary course of the firm's business when the accident occurred.

It is possible, of course, that one partner may commit a tort against another partner whilst in the ordinary course of business – for example where one partner is a passenger in a car driven by the other, and is injured as a result of the driver's negligence. Obviously, the wrongdoer is liable for his act, but here the law is unclear on whether liability extends to the whole firm.

Criminal liability

Traditionally, criminal liability is personal, and is based on the concept of individual guilt. For most offences the prosecutor must show that the accused had a guilty mind, or was negligent or grossly careless, and punishment follows from that. In these cases (which would cover the whole range of what would popularly be regarded as 'serious' offences, whether against persons or property) there is no sense in which a firm, or partners in general, can be directly punished for the crime of one partner. There might, of course, be indirect consequences, in terms of loss of goodwill.

Practically speaking, however, one of the main potential sources of criminal liability for a professional firm falls under the environmental, health and safety or food safety legislation. Most of these statutory offences carry 'strict liability', which means that the prosecution only has to show that the defendant committed the offence; punishment follows from that, and the defendant's intention, or lack of it, is irrelevant. In addition, the enforcement agency can select its own defendant from among the partners; it may choose the senior partner – to attract maximum publicity for the prosecution – or it may choose the partner whose department was responsible for the statutory breach. In this context, therefore, criminal liability is no longer 'personal' in the established sense.

It is interesting here to compare the position of the limited company. The company itself, as a legal person, may be prosecuted for these offences under the concept of strict liability. A company, of course, cannot realistically be said to have a guilty mind. Directors can, however, and under the Environmental Protection Act 1990, for example, there is also power to prosecute directors where individual guilt or negligence can be proved.

So, for example, the National Rivers Authority could prosecute a company for polluting a river and the directors can be prosecuted as well if, but only if, they had the necessary 'criminal' intention. With a partnership, on the other hand, the National Rivers Authority could prosecute one or more of the partners individually without having the additional burden of proving intention. For companies or partnerships the usual punishment will be a heavy fine (maximum £20,000 under the Environmental Protection Act 1990) but in particularly serious cases guilty individuals, not companies, may be imprisoned.

It will be apparent that partnerships are more exposed than limited companies in this area, specifically bearing in mind their unlimited liability. Indeed, where a firm's business carries particular risks of prosecution there may be an argument for incorporation on this ground alone (and see Chapter 12).

As a postscript, it is worth noting that the recent prosecution of P & O over the Zeebrugge ferry disaster finally established that it is possible to prosecute a company, through its directors, for manslaughter. This is an exception to the principles stated above, since manslaughter is an intentional crime and, in practice, such prosecutions, formidably expensive as they are, will be rare.

Criminal acts may also be torts: a firm which fails to keep a dangerous substance under lock and key, as required by the health and safety regulations, will be guilty of an offence but will also be liable to compensate an individual who is harmed by that substance. Damages for personal injuries can be very substantial.

Nature of the liability of partners

The 1890 Act drew a distinction between liability for contracts on the one hand and liability for civil or criminal wrongs on the other. In the case of liability for contracts each partner is liable *jointly* with his co-partners for obligations incurred whilst he was a partner. Strictly, this means that if a creditor obtains judgment against one or some of the partners in a firm he is barred from subsequently suing any of the others if the first judgment is unproductive. By contrast, all partners carry joint and several liability for civil or criminal wrongs, so that an individual claiming compensation for a wrongful act has the choice of suing each partner in turn, or the partners all together, until his full claim is met.

In 1978, however, the law was changed to allow a creditor who has been unable to execute a judgment against one partner to come back to court and seek judgment against the others. This means that the distinction between joint and several liability, although still to be found in the legislation, no longer carries any significance.

CHAPTER 6

Partnership Accounts

WHAT ARE PARTNERSHIP ACCOUNTS?

The term 'accounts' is used commercially in two senses:

(1) to describe the figures prepared by a business at regular intervals which summarise its trading for the accounting period and highlight the financial position at the end of the period; and

(2) to describe the books, ledgers or database maintained by a business to record its financial transactions. These are more accurately referred to as the 'accounting records'.

WHY ARE PARTNERSHIP ACCOUNTS NEEDED?

Unlike a company, which is required to submit accounts to the Registrar of Companies, for possible public inspection, a partnership is not legally obliged to provide financial statements. In practice, however, accounts and accounting records are essential, for a number of reasons.

(1) Accounts provide the necessary information to the Inland Revenue for income tax and PAYE and to HM Customs and Excise for VAT.

(2) Accounts give a financial overview of the business so that partners may have information about debts due to them and debts owed to creditors or to those who finance the business.

(3) Accounts are a valuable management tool which afford partners an insight into how their business is performing. They will be essential if the firm wishes to raise finance in the form of loans or overdraft facilities. Potential lenders will insist that the business has proper accounting systems in place so as to ensure that prompt and reliable financial information is always available. This means that, in turn, accounting records should be carefully

maintained at all times so as to allow the partners or their accountants to prepare accounts at the end of each accounting period.

As a firm grows and the volume of transactions increases more administrative time will be needed to maintain the accounting records. At some point the partners will need to consider the purchase of a micro-computer to run a standard software package which will be appropriate for the firm's accounting needs.

When considering the purchase of hardware and software packages, partners should consider not just the present accounting needs of the firm but also the type of management information which partners would like their accounting system to provide, plus the total human resource cost of implementing the package effectively. Before making any decisions it is essential that they discuss the matter with their accountants.

THE BASIC ACCOUNTING SYSTEM

The established technique for the maintenance of accounting records is known as the double-entry bookkeeping system. This is based on the understanding that every financial transaction has two aspects, and that both need to be recorded. For example, if a firm invoices a client, records kept under the double-entry book keeping system will show:

(1) an entry for fee income; and
(2) an entry showing that the client owes those fees to the partnership.

Subsequently, when the fees are paid, the records will show:

(1) the discharge of the amount owed by the client; and
(2) an increase in the firm's bank balance, reflecting the payment received.

The double-entry system splits transactions into debit entries and credit entries. These are commonly shown in a 'T' account in the following way.

Debit   Credit

| Transaction | £ | Transaction | £ |

By convention, debits are shown on the left-hand side and represent expenses and assets of the business. Credits are shown on the right-hand side, and represent income, liabilities and the partners' funding of the business.

Each transaction is recorded by a debit and a credit entry, which counterbalance each other. Consequently, at any given moment, the sum of all debits in the records will equal the sum of all credits.

Separate accounts should be maintained for the principal types of transactions of the business – for example for fee income, staff costs, and the operation of the firm's bank accounts.

WHAT ACCOUNTING RECORDS ARE NEEDED?

Whatever books are kept they should be comprehensive enough to record the following information:

(1) payments and receipts through the firm's bank account;
(2) invoices delivered by the firm;
(3) goods, equipment or services purchased by the firm.

All accounting records should be preserved for at least seven years after the period to which they relate. HM Customs and Excise may require details of the previous six years' accounts, and the Inland Revenue may go back for seven years.

PARTNERS' ACCOUNTS

The financial relationships between partners are usually recorded in three separate accounts: capital account; drawings account; and current account.

Capital account

Permanent, financial contributions from partners by way of cash or other assets will normally be required, and the partnership agreement should make provision for this. Where capital is contributed disproportionately, interest should be paid in order to maintain parity between partners. Where capital contributions are equal, interest may or may not be paid, depending on preference. The rate of interest on capital should be specified in the partnership agreement and will normally be equivalent to that payable on external borrowings.

Drawings account

As partners are not employees of the firm they do not pay themselves salaries as such. Instead, each partner will take regular cash drawings, which must not be shown as expenses of the firm and are therefore shown in the drawings account. This account will record all money drawn from the firm by partners and all expenses paid out on behalf of partners – for example National Insurance contributions, income tax and professional negligence premiums.

At each year end the balance on the drawings account will be transferred to the current account.

Note, in particular, that for the purposes of calculating income tax payable by a partner, drawings are not synonymous with income.

Current account

The current account reflects the investment by partners in the business other than by specific capital contributions. At the end of each financial year, profits made by the firm will be apportioned between the partners in the agreed profit-sharing ratio, and the relevant amounts will be credited to each partner's current account. Similarly, the balance on each partner's drawings account will be taken to his current account. The current account will not normally attract interest payments.

THE FORMAT OF THE ACCOUNTS

Whilst there is no prescribed format for the presentation of partnership accounts, they will generally be presented in accordance with accepted accounting practice. This means that the accounts will consist of:

(1) a balance sheet drawn up to the accounting reference date; and
(2) trading and profit and loss accounts for the accounting period.

Balance sheet

The balance sheet shows the assets and liabilities of the firm, together with the partners' own investment. The balance sheet may convey only basic information or can give considerable financial detail by means of added notes or appendices.

The basic information will be set out as follows.

	£	£
Fixed assets		XXX
Current assets		
work in progress	XXX	
client debtors	XXX	
pre-payments	XXX	
other debts	XXX	
cash at bank and in hand	XXX	
	XXXX	

Current liabilities	£	£
trade creditors	XXX	
other creditors	XXX	
accruals	XXX	
partners' current accounts	XXX	
	(XXXX)	
Net current assets		XXXX
Total assets less current liabilities		XXXX
Long-term liabilities		(XXXX)
Net assets		XXXX
Represented by partners' capital accounts		
Partner A		XXXX
Partner B		XXXX
Partner C		XXXX
		XXXX

FIXED ASSETS

The figure shown under 'fixed assets' represents the cost or valuation of all fixed assets of the firm, whether purchased by the firm or brought in by the partners. An allowance for depreciation is deducted and charged to the profit and loss account on an annual basis.

CURRENT ASSETS

Work in progress
The 'work in progress' figure represents the cost of any work in progress for customers or clients which has not yet been invoiced.

Client debtors
'Client debtors' are sales or fees invoiced to clients and represent the amounts owed to the firm, inclusive of VAT where relevant.

Pre-payments
Pre-payments (sometimes termed 'disbursements') cover services paid for in advance, or services which cover a period of time such as insurance or property rents. Where the benefit of expenditure extends into the future a proportion is carried forward to be shown as an expense in the future accounting period.

Cash at bank/in hand
Bank or building society balances and any petty cash which may be held at the year end will be taken into account under 'current assets'.

CURRENT LIABILITIES

Trade creditors
The figure for 'trade creditors' represents sums owing to the firm's suppliers.

Other creditors
'Other creditors' includes money owing to HM Customs and Excise in respect of VAT and to the Inland Revenue in respect of PAYE.

Accruals
'Accruals' are similar to pre-payments but represent expenses paid for in arrears, such as electricity, gas and telephone charges.

LONG-TERM LIABILITIES

Assets and liabilities which are 'current' will fall due or be recovered within 12 months. 'Long-term liabilities', on the other hand, encompass liabilities, such as term, bank loans and leases, which will fall due after more than one year.

Profit and loss account

The profit and loss account is a summary of all the partnership transactions during the accounting period. All amounts are shown exclusive of VAT, so that the accounts represent the actual cost to the partnership. The typical profit and loss account would be set out as follows.

	£	£
Sales		XXXX
Cost of sales		
opening stock/work-in-progress	XXX	
trade purchases	XXX	
	XXXX	
Less closing stock	(XXX)	XXXX
Gross profit		XXXX

Less overheads
 wages and NIC   XX
 rent and rates   XX
 insurance   XX
 telephone   XX
 motor expenses   XX
 printing and advertising   XX
 sundry expenses   XX
 depreciation   XX

                         XXX

Net profit for the period   XXX

Appropriation of profit

Partner	A	B
Salaries	XX	
Interest	X	X
50:50 apportionment	XX	XX
	XX	XX

SALES

'Sales' covers transactions during the accounting period, and includes work for which costs have not yet been recovered at the year end, or debtors.

COST OF SALES

'Cost of sales' are trade costs relating to sales made during the accounting period. 'Opening stock/work-in-progress', which is included in the cost of sales, means items purchased or work done in the previous accounting period which has been invoiced in the current period (in professional partnerships, work-in-progress will be the principal element). 'Closing stock', which is not included, relates to goods and services which have not yet been invoiced.

GROSS PROFIT

The 'gross profit' is an important figure in the profit and loss account. The ratio of gross profit to turnover is known as the 'gross margin' and is a key indicator to the firm's trading performance.

OVERHEADS

'Overheads' represent all other expenses of the running and administration of the business. Many of these costs will be of a fixed nature, for example rent, and will not vary directly with the level of partnership business. Overheads may be split into sub-categories, such as selling and distribution costs, establishment costs and finance costs.

NET PROFIT

The 'net profit' is the difference between the gross profit earned by the firm and the overheads incurred in achieving that profit. Unlike the gross margin, the net profit margin will not be stable, but will rise as the business increases. The objective of any successful business will, of course, be to keep its overheads down whilst increasing gross profit.

CHAPTER 7

Partnership Tax

INTRODUCTION

The object of this chapter is to provide an outline of the most important tax
rules relating to the general running of the partnership business. Tax planning
strategies for individual partners have not been included, and for these,
together with points of detail and the tax issues arising on more unusual
transactions, specialist advice will be essential.

For most (although not all) purposes, the tax treatment of partnerships
reflects the fact that in English law, a partnership is not recognised as a
separate, legal person from the partners. As a result, unlike the shareholders in
a company, the partners are treated as though they are collectively entitled to
the firm's income or assets, the firm being no more than the sum of the
partners.

In a consultative document ('A Simpler System for Assessing Personal Tax')
issued in November 1992, which follows and responds to an earlier consultative document, the Inland Revenue proposed a number of changes to the tax
system which would alter the way in which partnerships are taxed on their
business income. However, no date for introduction of any changes has yet
been set. For this reason the chapter deals with the present law and practice
only. If the proposals are implemented, this will substantially alter the present
system of income tax for partnerships. In particular, the cash-flow advantage
currently enjoyed by partners as a result of the preceding year basis of taxation
(see p 57 below) will be removed, and partners will be separately assessed on
their share of partnership profits, rather than these being the subject of a joint
assessment as at present.

Income receipts and chargeable gains

Unfortunately, there is no single authoritative test which can be applied to
decide whether a receipt of the firm is an income receipt, which may be subject

to income tax, or a capital receipt which may give rise to a charge to capital gains tax ('CGT'). The distinction between the two depends on case-law and on a detailed consideration of all the relevant circumstances. It should be noted that the accounting treatment of a transaction is not conclusive for tax purposes. A receipt may be treated as income for tax purposes, notwithstanding that it has been treated as capital in the firm's accounts and vice versa. The fact that payments are recurrent (annual or monthly, for example) tends to suggest that they are income, but, again, this is not conclusive; they may be instalments of a capital sum.

Happily, in most cases, the distinction will be straightforward. Income receipts will include receipts from sale of trading stock, payments for professional services, interest and rental income. Where the partnership disposes of premises, machinery and equipment used in its business or of other items treated for accounting purposes as fixed capital, the proceeds will normally be capital receipts. There will, however, be cases where the position is not clear-cut, and specialist advice may be desirable in relation to major transactions (particularly if the firm is intending to use a particular type of relief or allowance to shelter the profits from tax) or where the tax treatment hinges on the precise nature and circumstances of the transaction. Receipts which should be considered carefully include compensation payments, payments for intellectual property, restrictive covenants or other contracts relating to the conduct of the firm's business, and payments to the firm on sale of, or under the terms of, traded securities, futures, options or similar derivative instruments.

INCOME TAX ★★★

For partnerships, as for individuals and companies, the basis on which income is taxed depends on the category, or 'Schedule' into which it falls. It is computed and assessed under the rules which apply to that Schedule, which also determine the reliefs available to set against the income. Some Schedules are further subdivided into 'Cases', which have their own rules for computation and assessment.

Partnerships will normally carry on a trade or profession and will derive most of their income from this. Trading income and professional income are taxed under Schedule D, Case I and Schedule D, Case II respectively, but for most purposes the rules applicable to Case I and Case II income are very similar. Income from a vocation is also taxed under Case II, so that the distinction between a profession and vocation is normally immaterial for tax purposes. For convenience, this chapter will generally only refer to professions, but the same rules will apply in the rare case of a partnership carrying on a vocation.

It should not be assumed, however, that *all* income of a partnership which carries on a trade or profession will be taxed under Schedule D: this only applies to income which arises directly out of the trade or profession. If it is income which arises out of an office or employment it will be taxed under Schedule E, in the hands of the partner to whom it was paid. For example, payments made to medical practitioners or dentists under part-time NHS contracts are Schedule E payments, as are, strictly speaking, fees paid to partners acting as company directors. The Inland Revenue may, by concession, tax small payments in this category under Schedule D. Since Schedule D offers fiscal advantages to a firm, the tax position should always be clarified before partners accept new offices which, albeit beneficial for the firm's business as a whole, may not necessarily be regarded as arising directly out of it.

A firm may also have income from rent (perhaps from a sub-letting of part of the firm's premises) which is taxable under Schedule A, or income from partnership investments, which is taxable under Schedule D, Case III.

Schedule D, Cases I and II

BASIS OF ASSESSMENT

In general, liability to income tax is assessed for each tax year (also called the 'year of assessment'). The tax year runs from 6 April in one year to 5 April in the next. For some categories of income (for example income from employment which is taxed under Schedule E) the amount of income assessed in each tax year is simply the income which arises in the tax year in question.

Income within Schedule D, Cases I and II is, however, at present assessed to tax on a basis normally referred to as the 'preceding year basis'. For each tax year the assessable trading or professional income is the income which arose in the accounting period ending in the *previous* tax year. The preceding year basis of assessment gives the taxpayer a cashflow advantage, and takes account of the fact that a firm will normally make up yearly accounts for an accounting period which may not coincide with the tax year.

Example

A trading partnership makes up its accounts to 31 December in every year. Its Schedule D, Case I profits were £100,000 for the year ending 31 December 1990 and £120,000 for the year ending 31 December 1991.

For the tax year 1991–92 the profits assessable to tax will be £100,000 (ie the profits for the accounting period ending 31 December 1990, because that date falls in the tax year 1990–91).

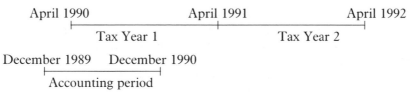

Normally the tax due will be payable in two equal instalments, the first on 1 January 1992 and the second on 1 July 1992.

The example shows that the tax on the firm's trading or professional profits will always be due substantially after the period in which the profits arose. The earlier in the tax year the firm's accounting period ends, the greater will be the benefit. An accounting period coinciding with the tax year is the least efficient choice. Maximum deferment is obtained by having an accounting period ending on 6 April. If the firm would prefer to make up its accounts to the end of a calendar month, 30 April may be a convenient date to choose.

Where the firm's profits are rising, the deferment will mean that in each tax year the firm is paying tax on profits which are lower than those it is currently realising. Conversely, if profits are in decline, the payment of the tax on the earlier profits may be a real burden for the firm, especially if money has not been earmarked to meet the liability.

Opening and closing year rules
Special rules apply to the first three tax years after the firm begins a new trade or profession and for the last three years in which it carries on a trade or profession. The rules which apply to these 'opening' and 'closing' years are explained below. They are also relevant when there is a change in the partnership, such as the retirement or death of a partner, or the introduction of a new partner.

COMPUTING SCHEDULE D, CASES I AND II PROFITS FOR TAX PURPOSES

Profit and loss account
The starting point in arriving at the firm's taxable trading or professional profits will be its profit and loss account (see p 52). This may be prepared, broadly, on an earnings basis, a cash basis or, in the case of a professional partnership, a bills delivered basis. The Inland Revenue may accept use of any of these bases for tax purposes, but its preference is for an earnings basis. This will normally be the only acceptable basis in the case of a trade and will also be required for at least the three opening years of a professional partnership.

The Inland Revenue will always permit the adoption of an earnings basis in place of any other basis, but their view is that once such a change has been made, it is final.

Adjustments to profits for tax purposes

The figures in the profit and loss account may have to be adjusted to exclude items of expenditure which are not deductible for tax purposes and to take account of receipts deemed to arise under specific statutory provisions.

Among the items of expenditure which the partnership cannot deduct in computing Schedule D, Cases I or II profits are:

(1) capital expenditure (even if, as a matter of accounting practice, this is written off against income over a period of years); relief may be available for some capital expenditure in the form of capital allowances;

(2) 'Salaries' and interest on partnership capital paid to partners (see p 49) since these items are, in reality, part of the profits; payments to salaried partners who are employees are deductible (see p 93);

(3) expenditure not incurred wholly and exclusively for the purposes of the trade or profession in question; and

(4) expenditure which falls within the scope of specific statutory provisions which preclude relief.

Expenditure not incurred 'wholly and exclusively' for the purposes of the trade or profession

Broadly, 'wholly' in this context is taken to relate to the amount of the expenditure, and 'exclusively' to the purpose for which it is incurred. Expenditure incurred purely for personal purposes cannot, of course, be set against business profits. Relief will also be refused, however, for expenditure incurred for *both* business *and* personal purposes, even if the business purpose was predominant. Expenditure will normally be treated as incurred for personal purposes, to some extent at least, where the person carrying on the business derives any personal benefit from the expenditure; it is only if it can be demonstrated that the personal benefit is a purely incidental and inevitable by-product of expenditure which was incurred for business purposes that a deduction will be available.

In the case of a partnership, it is the partners who run the business. Accordingly, expenditure which, except incidentally, confers a personal benefit on one or more of the partners will not be deductible. It is not open to the firm to argue that such expenditure is deductible because the partners believe it was incurred in the interests of the firm at large.

This point was settled in a case which related to removal expenses and disturbance allowances paid to partners in a large accountancy firm who were required to relocate in the interests of the firm's business. The House of Lords accepted that the payments were intended to ensure that partners were more willing to relocate when required to do so, but held that the immediate purpose of the payments was related to the provision of private accommodation for individual partners. A sole practitioner would not have been entitled to relief for expenditure on his private accommodation and, in their view, the position was not changed simply because the partnership was a large one and the decision to make the payments was not confined to the partners who benefited from them. (By contrast, a company paying removal expenses to a director required to relocate for business purposes would normally be entitled to a deduction.)

Items of expenditure for which no relief is available on the ground that they are incurred to serve a personal need of the partner, or confer a private benefit on him include:

– the cost of travel from home to work, save in the rare situation where the partner works from home;

– expenditure on meals for partners at partnership meetings;

– the cost of private medical treatment;

– the cost of defending a partner against criminal proceedings;

– charitable donations unless made by covenant or under the Gift Aid scheme, although the costs of sponsorship may be deductible on the same basis as advertising costs.

Specific items of deductible expenditure worth noting:
– the cost of accommodation and, surprisingly, also of meals where provided at a residential course or conference attended for business purposes;

– the cost of travel between places of work;

– the cost of travel, accommodation and food on trips undertaken solely for business purposes and with no 'holiday' element for the partner or members of his family, on the basis that any personal benefit is purely incidental;

– subscriptions to an appropriate professional body;

– rent, including rent payable to a partner at a normal commercial rate and on a normal commercial basis;

– premiums for indemnity insurance and insurance of trading stock, premises and business equipment;

– interest on business loans; and

– salaries paid to partners' spouses or other relatives (which can be a useful way of ensuring that a spouse's personal allowance and lower-rate tax band, effective from 1992–93, are fully utilised, but payments will only be deductible to the extent that they reflect genuine contributions to the firm).

As a matter of strict law there is probably no provision for the apportionment of a particular item of expenditure between business and non-business purposes. In practice, however, the Inland Revenue will often allow a deduction to be made for a proportion of expenditure incurred on running a car used for both business and personal purposes corresponding with the proportion of business use. The same applies to electricity, gas and telephone bills where a partner works from home.

Staff costs, including wages, National Insurance contributions and the provision of fringe benefits and training for staff, will normally have been incurred exclusively for the purposes of the firm's business, which will be served, for example, by the attraction and retention of good staff. Special care may be needed in the area of ex gratia payments, such as 'golden handshakes' to staff, or if the firm wishes to make lump-sum payments which will be tax free in the hands of the recipient. Professional advice should be taken if the sums involved are substantial.

Expenditure for which relief is precluded by statute
For most partnerships the most important category of expenditure for which relief is prohibited by statute is business entertainment expenditure. Even where the cost of entertainment or hospitality is incurred wholly and exclusively for business purposes, it will normally not be deductible unless provided for bona fide members of staff. Similarly, the cost of gifts to business clients is generally not deductible, although there is an exception for small gifts of articles other than food, drink, tobacco, tokens and vouchers. The exception will only apply if the article incorporates a conspicuous advertisement for the firm and the total value of such articles given by the firm to the recipient in that tax year is £10 or less.

Expenditure for which relief is available by specific statutory provision: loans to purchase a share in a partnership
In addition to the general principles set out above, there are certain types of expenditure for which relief is specifically provided by statute. The most important of these in the context of a partnership is relief on a loan taken out to buy a partnership share or provide partnership capital.

Capital allowances
Where the firm has incurred expenditure on certain types of capital asset, including plant and machinery, patents or know-how and scientific research, capital allowances may be available.

A full discussion of the scheme of allowances is outside the scope of this chapter, but partners should be aware that the term 'plant' is very broad and would include, for example, the professional library required to set up in business, or equipment for a surgery.

ASSESSMENT OF SCHEDULE D, CASES I AND II PROFITS; DIVIDING THE ASSESSMENT

Schedule D, Cases I and II profits are usually covered by a single partnership assessment which will be apportioned between the partners according to their

profit share *for the tax year to which the assessment relates*. The amount of the
assessment is a partnership debt, for which the partners are jointly (though not
severally) liable. This means that the Inland Revenue is entitled to claim the
whole of the tax assessed from any one of the partners, although that partner
would have a right to recover the appropriate proportion of the tax paid from
the others. If one of the partners becomes bankrupt, however, the others may
be compelled to bear his share of the tax bill. This is one reason why it is
important for the firm to retain enough of its profits to meet the partnership
assessment before the surplus is distributed.

Reliefs available to individual partners

Each partner can deduct the reliefs and allowances to which he is entitled from
his share of the partnership assessment unless these have been absorbed by
other income, such as interest on personal investments. In practice, most
partners find it convenient to set all their allowances against their share of the
partnership assessment, and it will normally be possible to agree this with the
Inland Revenue, unless another source of income would otherwise be com-
pletely covered by allowances (for example where a partner has a small amount
of investment income which would be covered wholly by his personal allowance).

Expenses incurred by individual partners

As already explained, revenue expenses incurred by individual partners wholly
and exclusively for the purposes of the business are deductible in computing
the partnership's assessable profits in the same way as expenses paid through
the partnership accounts. They cannot, of course, also be set against individual
partners' shares of the assessment as this would mean relief being given twice
for the same expense.

Partnership losses

Loss relief is a complex area of tax law, and professional advice should be taken
with a view to obtaining maximum relief for losses at the earliest possible date.
This should also ensure that the elections required for some types of loss relief
are made within the statutory time-limits. Essentially, losses will be borne by
partners in accordance with their partnership agreement. A partner may elect
to set off his share of a loss against income from other sources (including capital
gains) of the same or the next tax year, or may choose to carry it forward to set
against future profits of the trade or profession.

Opening and closing year rules

The normal rules which at present provide for assessment of profits under
Cases I and II of Schedule D on a preceding year basis are superseded by
special rules in the opening or closing years of a trade or profession. These rules
apply to individuals as well as partnerships. In the case of partnerships,
however, they need to be considered not only where a trade or profession is
actually commenced or discontinued, but also where there is a change in the

partnership, since this may result in the partnership's trade or profession being *deemed* to cease and recommence.

Opening year rules

For the tax year in which a trade or profession is commenced, tax is due on the actual profits realised between the commencement date and the end of the tax year on 5 April. For the following tax year, tax is due on the actual profits realised during the calendar year from the date the trade/profession first starts.

In the third tax year, and thereafter, the normal preceding year basis may apply. However, the firm may not have made up accounts for a twelve month period ending in the second tax year either because the business has not been running long enough, or because it has made up accounts for a shorter or longer period. In that case the firm will be assessed for the third tax year on the profits realised in the twelve months up to its accounting date (or intended accounting date) or, if this is impossible, the first twelve months' profits again, as in the second tax year.

Example

A partnership began to practise a new profession on 1 January 1992. It makes up its accounts to 30 June each year and its taxable profits are as follows:

1 January 1992	– 30 June 1992	£ 50,000
1 July 1992	– 30 June 1993	£120,000
1 July 1993	– 30 June 1994	£150,000

The firm would be assessed to tax on its profits as set out below.

First tax year: 6 April 1991 – 5 April 1992

Actual profits to 5 April 1992:
$$\frac{3\% \times £50,000}{6}$$
$$= £26,387$$

Second tax year: 6 April 1992 – 5 April 1993

Actual profits 1 January 1992 – 31 Dec 1992:
$$£50,000 + \frac{6}{12} \times £120,000$$
$$= £110,000$$

Third tax year: 6 April 1993 – 5 April 1994

First 12 months' profits: £110,000

(In principle, profits for the third and subsequent tax years are taxed on a normal, preceding year basis. But here there are no accounts for a 12-month period ending in the tax year 1992–93. The first 12 months' profits are, therefore, used again.)

Fourth tax year: 6 April 1994 – 5 April 1995

Profits for 12-month accounting
period ending in tax year 1993–94:   £120,000

Taxpayer's right to be taxed on actual profits
A firm may give notice to its Inspector of Taxes that for the second and third tax
years in which the profession is carried on it wishes to be taxed on the actual
profits realised, instead of being taxed on the basis explained above. The notice
has to apply to both years, and must be given within seven years of the end of
the second tax year.

    This alternative basis of assessment will normally reduce the firm's assess-
able profits if its actual profits (after adjustment for tax purposes) have fallen. It
should be noted, however, that a lower overall assessment will not always result
in lower tax bills for individual partners. That will depend additionally on how
the assessment is divided between partners, and the reliefs available to them.

Special relief for losses in opening years
In addition to the general reliefs for trading losses there is a special form of relief
for trading or professional losses incurred in the tax year when the business
commenced and in the following three tax years. This may entitle a partner to
carry back his share of the loss against any income assessable in the three years
preceding the year of the loss.

Closing year rules
Special rules also apply when a firm discontinues its trade or profession. In the
tax year when this happens the firm is taxed on its actual profits from the start of
the tax year on 6 April to the date the trade or profession ceases.

    In the two previous tax years, the basic rule is that the firm is assessed on the
normal preceding year basis. If, however, an assessment based on the actual
aggregate profits for those two years would be higher, the Inland Revenue is
required to use that method.

Example

A partnership which made up its accounts to 5 May each year ceased to carry on
business on 5 October 1991. It had realised taxable profits as follows:

6 May 1987 – 5 May 1988	£100,000
6 May 1988 – 5 May 1989	£120,000
6 May 1989 – 5 May 1990	£150,000
6 May 1990 – 5 May 1991	£ 30,000
6 May 1991 – 5 October 1991	£ 5,000

The firm's profits assessable to tax on the two alternative methods will be as set
out below (in reverse chronological order).

Tax year 1991–92: final year

£5,000 + $\frac{1}{12}$ × £30,000   No alternative

= £7,500

Tax year 1990–91: penultimate year

Preceding year basis   Actual basis

£120,000 $\frac{11}{12}$ × £30,000 + $\frac{1}{12}$ × £150,000

          = £40,000

Tax year 1989–90: ante-penultimate year

Preceding year basis   Actual basis

£100,000 $\frac{11}{12}$ × £150,000 + $\frac{1}{12}$ × £120,000

          = £147,500

Clearly the profits here would be assessed on the preceding year basis because the assessable profits for the tax years 1989–90 and 1990–91 would be lower in aggregate if the actual basis was used.

Terminal loss relief
There are special rules here allowing partners to carry back losses incurred in the final 12 months of business. These match the opening year loss rules already referred to.

Work in progress and post-cessation receipts
As might be expected there are rules for valuing work in progress when a business is discontinued, and for bringing into account sums received by the firm after discontinuance.

CHANGES IN THE PARTNERSHIP ★★★

The rules outlined above are important because they will be relevant not only when a partnership is first set up, or ceases business, but also whenever there is any change in the composition of the firm. The Taxes Acts regard such a change as a 'deemed discontinuance'; for tax purposes the firm is treated as though the business had been permanently discontinued and a new business commenced at the date of the partnership change. Examples of relevant changes would be:

– where one or more partners joins an existing partnership, or where a salaried partner becomes an equity partner;

– where one or more partners leaves a continuing partnership (whether on retirement, on death or for some other reason);

– where a sole practitioner takes on one or more partners;

– where a partnership is dissolved on the departure of one or more partners, leaving a sole practitioner carrying on the firm's business.

Where a deemed discontinuance occurs, partners have a choice. They may elect to have the business treated as continuing for tax purposes, or they may do nothing, in which case the business will be treated by the Inland Revenue as having closed. All partners, new and old, must make the election. Generally speaking, a continuation election will be in most partners' best interests and it is important, therefore, to seek advice from the firm's advisers at an early stage, particularly as the election has to be made within two years of the partnership change. If, as sometimes happens, individual partners are prejudiced by a decision which is in the interests of the majority, it may be reasonable for the firm to make 'equity adjustments' between the gainers and losers. Such arrangements are less painful if a firm has previously adopted the practice of creating tax reserves in the firm's accounts. The partnership agreement should address this issue by stipulating that partners will sign an election where this is judged to benefit the firm as a whole, and by making provision to compensate partners who are disadvantaged as a result (see p 30).

CAPITAL GAINS TAX　★★★

Capital gains tax is complex, and may provide a trap for the unwary, especially the unwary partner. It is capable of affecting all straightforward dispositions of property – by sale or gift for example – but, in addition, it is relevant whenever there is a change in the constitution of a partnership. A detailed discussion of the relevant rules lies beyond the scope of this book, and those in partnership should always plan for the adjustment of assets or partnership shares on the admission of a new partner, in conjunction with their tax advisers. It should also be noted that the Inland Revenue have published Statements of Practice to try to produce workable solutions to some of the problems outlined below.

Basic principles

Disposals of assets by way of sale or gift may attract capital gains tax. At present capital gains are taxed as the top slice of an individual's income; if the total of his income and gains exceeds the top of the basic rate band (£23,700 for 1993/94), that excess will be taxed at the same rate as higher rate income tax, which is currently 40 per cent.

Certain assets are specifically exempted from the charge to capital gains tax. The most important of these are an individual's main residence, cars, most sterling securities and moveable assets with an expected life of less than 50 years (but excluding certain assets on which capital allowances have been or could have been claimed).

The tax is aimed at capital profits and, consequently, a chargeable gain (or loss) is calculated by deducting from the proceeds of disposal of an asset expenditure previously incurred in respect of it (often referred to as the 'base cost'). Allowable expenditure includes, broadly, the original cost of the asset, money spent with a view to enhancing its value and the costs of disposing of it. Where assets are given away or disposed of other than commercially, their market value may replace proceeds of sale in the computation.

There is an extensive scheme of reliefs and allowances which may reduce or eliminate a chargeable gain. In particular, if a gain arises on the retirement of a partner he may be entitled to retirement relief. Professional advice should always be taken to ensure that this, and other reliefs, are fully utilised.

Disposal of partnership assets ★★★

As we have seen (at Chapter 4) partnerships do not have the capacity to own property because they lack legal personality. For capital gains tax purposes, therefore, each partner is regarded as owning a fraction of the value of the partnership assets. This has the following consequences:

– where capital assets are disposed of, each individual partner, not the firm as a whole, is treated as making a disposal which may give rise to a taxable gain;

– when a partner disposes of, or reduces his share of, the firm's assets (for example on retirement, or when the firm takes in a new partner) he may also realise a taxable gain;

– when a partner acquires a share of the assets, or enlarges his share, he will make an acquisition for tax purposes;

– in addition, partners are 'connected persons', so that transactions between them are not regarded as being conducted at arm's length, or commercially. This means that, in calculating capital gains, a market valuation is substituted for the actual consideration that passes – so adding further complications.

All this contrasts with the much more straightforward position of a shareholder in a limited company, who is treated as owning only his shares, not an equivalent slice of the company's assets, and who is, therefore, subject to tax only on a disposal of those shares.

Capital gains tax forms part of each partner's own tax assessment. Capital gains (or losses) realised by each partner in his capacity as a partner are treated in exactly the same way as gains or losses on his personal investments.

INHERITANCE TAX

Inheritance tax is charged on transfers of value by individuals. A transfer of value is any transfer which reduces the value of the transferor's estate. Essentially, the tax is directed at gifts or the conferring of gratuitous benefits, not commercial deals and is not, therefore, attracted by transactions between persons engaged in a business relationship.

An individual may make many different transfers of value during his lifetime and, when he dies, he is *treated* as having made a transfer of value equivalent to the value of the whole of his estate at that time. The tax is cumulative and is payable, after death, on the aggregate value of all lifetime transfers which have not been exempted from tax, plus the deemed transfer on death. The first £150,000 (1993/94 figures) is free of tax ('nil rate band') and, above that, tax is chargeable at 40 per cent.

The majority of lifetime transfers are potentially exempt from tax ('PETS'). This means that if the transferor survives a particular transfer by seven years or more, no tax will be payable.

Implications for partnerships   ★★★

As with capital gains tax, problems may arise because a firm is treated, for tax purposes, as a collection of individuals engaged in a relationship which is not necessarily a truly commercial one ('connected persons'). Consequently, the transfer of a share in a partnership, on the death of a partner or otherwise, may be taken to be a transfer of value for inheritance tax purposes, and it will then be up to the partners to show that the internal transaction in question has been conducted on a market basis, without any element of gratuitous benefit.

In practice, however, the availability of business property relief does substantially mitigate these problems. Once again, discussion of the finer points has to be omitted here, but it will be apparent that advice needs to be taken on potential inheritance tax liability in respect of all internal transactions and, in particular, when drafting provisions of the partnership agreement which allow partners to acquire an individual's share on his retirement or death.

VALUE ADDED TAX   ★★

Value added tax ('VAT') is collected and controlled by HM Customs and Excise, an entirely separate body from the Inland Revenue. It is charged on the taxable supply of goods or services by a 'taxable person' in the course of a business and, for this one fiscal purpose, a partnership will be equated with a limited company and treated as a taxable person. This means that the VAT registration will be in the firm's name but, in addition, the names of all partners will have to be supplied to the Commissioners of Customs and Excise, and there is a further requirement to notify the Commissioners of changes in the composition of the firm, or even changes in the names or addresses of partners. This highlights the fact that the principle of joint liability between partners applies to a VAT debt as to any other.

A firm will be obliged to register for VAT if it is making 'taxable supplies' of goods or services, and, very broadly, if its turnover is above the prescribed VAT threshold (currently £37,600 per year). A good deal of service provision is exempt from VAT. Medical, dental, educational and financial services are all exempt and, therefore, non-taxable. Consequently, many professional partnerships will not be in a position to register for VAT, although they may be paying the tax on services or supplies which are purchased for the business.

VAT is charged either at zero rate (as, for example, on the supply of drugs on prescription) or at a standard rate, which is currently 17.5 per cent.

Once a firm is registered, VAT must be added to all invoices (even if it is shown at nil for a zero-rated supply). A firm which makes a taxable supply must account to the Commissioners for VAT on those services (output tax) but is entitled, before doing so, to offset tax paid in respect of goods or services purchased by it (allowable input tax). Firms making zero-rated supplies are, consequently, in an advantageous position fiscally because they do not have to charge VAT on their services, but, nevertheless, may set off input tax which they have to pay.

HM Customs and Excise have a team of inspectors who make regular visits to registered businesses. In general, the VAT regime is seen as far more stringent than that which operates in respect of direct taxes, and there are strict penalties for late registration, submission of late returns and under-declaration. This is an area where much care is needed, and professional advice will often be required.

CHAPTER 8

Endings

'In my beginning is my end.' (T S Eliot)

INTRODUCTION

Putting an end to a partnership can be a messy and emotional business. The analogy with marriage and its termination is strong: the relationship may be lightly entered into, but its death throes may be protracted and, often, highly contentious. For a professional partnership the winding-up may be the culmination of years of ill-feeling, distrust and a gradual fragmentation of goodwill between partners. It is hardly surprising, then, that every last financial detail may be a source of dispute.

That is not to say that all endings are problematic. Technically, there is a dissolution of one partnership and the immediate formation of another whenever one partner retires or a new partner is admitted to the firm. These events have tax consequences (see Chapter 7) but the partnership business, in most circumstances, continues unchanged. The same is usually true when a partner dies. On the other hand, a serious dispute between partners is likely to lead to a dissolution of the relationship *and* a winding-up of the business itself.

In this chapter we will consider the following issues:

– the circumstances in which a *general* dissolution and consequent winding-up will occur;

– the practical consequences of winding up; and

– the particular consequences of the death of a partner – an event which is likely to affect even the most compatible partnerships at one time or another.

DISSOLUTION IN GENERAL

Since partnerships are based in contract they may be ended by agreement. As we have seen (at Chapter 3), the partnership agreement itself may, and indeed

71

should, specify circumstances in which the partnership is to be dissolved. For example, it is very likely that a professional partnership, where reputation is important, will be subject to dissolution if a partner is guilty of professional misconduct. The Partnership Act 1890 ('the 1890 Act') is in the background here, however, and lays down five sets of circumstances in which a dissolution will *automatically* take place. The important point to note is that, if the partnership agreement specifically addresses these issues in a different way from the 1890 Act, then, with one exception, the operation of the 1890 Act is excluded.

Beyond this, whatever the partnership agreement says, it is open to any partner to apply to the court for a dissolution order. The grounds for so doing are again laid down in the 1890 Act, but the difference here is that dissolution is not automatic – the court will have to adjudicate on the matter and exercise its discretion.

Dissolution by agreement

As already indicated, partnerships may always be dissolved by mutual agreement of the partners. So, whatever the original planned duration of a partnership, or the original purpose of the partnership, the partners can always agree to end it prematurely. Dissolution in these circumstances must, however, be the result of a unanimous decision, unless the partnership agreement itself allows for a majority vote.

The partnership agreement may contain an express power to dissolve the partnership (see p 31). When circumstances arise which trigger the dissolution clause the procedures laid down in that clause must be observed. Usually this means that notice of dissolution will have to be given.

Cessation of business

If a partnership ceases to carry on business the inference must be that the partners have agreed to wind the business up. Without a 'business' there can be no partnership within the meaning of the 1890 Act.

AUTOMATIC DISSOLUTION UNDER THE 1890 ACT

Whenever any of the circumstances listed below occur, dissolution of the firm will be automatic. The partnership agreement may, however, override these criteria in all except case (5) below.

(1) Time

A partnership may be entered into for a defined period. This is the exception rather than the rule, but when it happens the 1890 Act provides that, subject to contrary agreement, the partnership will be dissolved when that period comes to an end.

In the same way, if a partnership is formed with a view to engaging in a particular transaction (for example a single publishing venture), the relationship will come to an end once that transaction has been completed unless, again, the partnership agreement otherwise specifies.

If a partnership is continued, by agreement, after the original agreed termination date, it will be known as 'a partnership at will'. This means that it may subsequently be ended at any time on notice being given by one of the partners to the others. This consequence is probably undesirable. It adds an element of unpredictability, in that the termination date will never be certain and, in the meantime, clauses in the original partnership agreement which are inconsistent with the concept of a partnership at will, are liable to be overridden. An example here would be a clause in the original agreement which precludes determination of the partnership by notice; this would be incompatible with a partnership at will, whose duration depends on notice.

(2) Notice

Some partnerships are created as partnerships at will, ie there is no agreed, fixed period for the duration of the partnership. In these circumstances any partner may dissolve the partnership at any time by giving appropriate notice.

The notice itself needs to be clear, unambiguous, and preferably in writing, so that there will be evidence of the terms if a dispute should arise later on. The length of notice may be specified in the partnership agreement, but otherwise the law does not require that reasonable notice has to be given. So a partnership may, in fact, be dissolved instantly, an outcome which, in most circumstances, is highly undesirable.

(3) Death or bankruptcy

In the absence of agreement to the contrary, the death of a partner will bring the partnership to an end from the date of death. This will be so even where the partnership was originally entered into for a specific period which has not yet come to an end.

Similarly, unless otherwise agreed, the bankruptcy of any partner will dissolve the partnership from the date of the bankruptcy order. There is a brief discussion of insolvency procedures in Chapter 9.

Generally speaking, it will be inconvenient for a modern partnership to subject itself to dissolution every time a partner dies or becomes insolvent. It will usually be much more satisfactory to value that partner's share and provide in the partnership agreement for some means of sorting things out without necessarily winding up the business.

(4) Charging order on a partner's share

If a partner's share of the partnership assets has been charged by the court with repayment of a separate personal debt, the other partners may opt to dissolve the partnership within a reasonable period after the date of the charging order. It seems that *all* the other partners must so opt if dissolution is to take place, and dissolution dates from that decision.

(5) Illegality   ★★

Where illegality occurs, dissolution really *is* automatic; partners may *not* avoid this rule by contrary provision in the partnership agreement.

The rule is that if any event occurs which makes it unlawful for the business of the firm to be carried on, or for the members of the firm to continue to be in partnership with one another, the partnership is dissolved. This will be the case even if the partners are unaware of the illegality in question.

A partnership will be illegal if it is formed for an illegal purpose, or if it is the intention of the partners that the purpose should be attained in an illegal way, for example a partnership formed to commit or benefit from a criminal offence is clearly illegal. A professional partnership will be illegal if it exceeds the numerical limits imposed by law (usually 20) and mixed or 'impure' partnerships will also be illegal. In a recent case, a firm of solicitors was dissolved where a partner forgot to renew his practising certificate; the same would be true where a partner in a dental practice ceased to be registered under the Dentists Act 1984.

DISSOLUTION BY THE COURT   ★★★

There are five grounds on which the court may dissolve a partnership. Clearly, this will be a last resort for partners, in a situation where the partnership agreement cannot provide an answer to their dispute and where a negotiated settlement cannot be reached. Legal advice is essential.

The grounds

(1) PERMANENT INCAPACITY

The court can dissolve a partnership where a partner becomes permanently incapable of fulfilling his role as partner. Any proceedings under this head must be initiated by a partner other than the one who is incapacitated.

Incapacity may be mental or physical. With mental incapacity the court may sometimes have to operate under the Mental Health Act 1983, rather than the 1890 Act. Where incapacity is physical the issue will be whether the incapacity actually *does* prevent the partner from fulfilling his role in the firm. Clearly, the court will have to look at his duties within the partnership, so that if he is, for example, a dormant or sleeping partner any incapacity is unlikely to have an appreciable effect on his function. Medical evidence of the extent of disability and of prognosis will usually be required.

(2) PREJUDICIAL CONDUCT

Where a partner is guilty of conduct which is calculated to prejudice the business, the court may dissolve the partnership at the request of another partner or the other partners. The nature of the business is relevant here. The sexual adventures of a partner in a trading business may, for example, be less likely to cause the court concern than an affair between a GP and his patient. On the other hand, there is no requirement for prejudicial conduct to be directly connected with the business, nor is there any need for the applicant to prove actual loss or public knowledge. The court simply has to judge the extent to which the clients or customers who knew of the conduct would have taken their business elsewhere.

(3) PERSISTENT BREACHES OF THE PARTNERSHIP AGREEMENT

The court may dissolve a partnership where a partner wilfully or persistently breaks the partnership agreement or conducts himself in such a way that it is not practicable for the other partners to continue a professional relationship with him. The court has to be able to distinguish between petty quarrels between partners and a state of affairs which has led to an irretrievable breakdown in internal relationships. Such conduct could be violent, dishonest, or simply disruptive.

(4) CARRYING ON THE BUSINESS AT A LOSS

Since partnership is a relationship which exists for the purpose of making profits, there must always be the expectation of profit. If it is clear that the business can only be continued at a loss, any partner is entitled to ask the court to dissolve the relationship. In these circumstances, proof of actual insolvency is unnecessary.

(5) THE JUST AND EQUITABLE GROUND

Finally, the court may dissolve a partnership where the purpose for which the partnership is formed can no longer be attained and dissolution is not available under one of the other grounds already mentioned. This is, in other words, a 'catch-all' ground and the court has considerable discretion in applying it. There is a counterpart of this provision in company law and it is clear from decided cases that the court will look for evidence which indicates a breakdown of the mutual confidence and trust which are, or should be, at the heart of the relationship between partners.

What about arbitration?

If the partnership agreement contains an arbitration clause the partnership disputes should go to arbitration and not to court. If a partner applies to the court for a dissolution and there is an arbitration clause, those who wish to avoid the publicity of court proceedings should seek immediate advice regarding an application to stay the hearing and refer to arbitration.

RETIREMENT OF A PARTNER ★★★

A partner has no 'right' to retire as such. The legal starting point here is that, since partnership is a relationship between individuals, that relationship is fundamentally changed if one of them leaves the firm. Consequently, dissolution will follow retirement unless there is an agreement that the remaining partner/s will continue to run the business afterwards. Dissolution, in these circumstances, is likely to have a disastrous effect on goodwill, and so it is most important that the partnership agreement should deal with the retirement of partners.

Agreements commonly provide for a partner to retire on giving written notice to his fellow partners. In addition, there are likely to be provisions indicating how the retiring partner's share of the business assets is to be valued.

Nowadays it is quite usual for partners to be required to retire on attaining a specified age; and in medical and dental partnerships practising within the National Health Service, retirement from practice is compulsory on attaining the age of 70. A clause intended to prevent a retiring partner from carrying on a competing business is also frequently found in partnership agreements. Restrictions of this nature must be 'reasonable' otherwise they are unenforceable; in drafting such clauses it is usually best to err on the side of caution, and legal advice should always be sought.

If there is no retirement clause in the partnership agreement a partner may become locked into a firm from which his fellow partners are unwilling to release him. In such cases his only legitimate option may be to seek dissolution of the partnership by the court. Sometimes, a disaffected partner may simply walk out. In these circumstances the remaining partners are usually well-advised to seek a negotiated settlement, since there will be little point in pursuing theoretical remedies.

WINDING-UP THE PARTNERSHIP AFFAIRS

Consequences of dissolution

On dissolution the partnership ceases to be a going concern. The next step is to wind up the business, which involves collecting in and valuing the assets, paying off debts, and distributing any surplus to the former partners.

In most cases the partners themselves will deal with the winding-up and their authority to bind the firm (see Chapter 5) will continue during the winding-up period. They will have power to pay debts, withdraw money deposited and sell partnership assets. Partners should complete work in progress, but they should not take on any new work unless it is necessary in order to facilitate a sale of the business.

Staff contracts of employment terminate on dissolution, and the firm will be liable for redundancy payments.

THE RETURN OF PREMIUMS

A premium is like an entry fee paid by a new partner to the others, and it is distinguished from a payment of capital made as an investment in the business. Premiums are uncommon these days, but where they have been paid, they are usually dealt with first on a winding-up.

The general rule expressed by the 1890 Act is that a partner who has paid a premium can recover all, or an appropriate amount of it, on a winding-up. The court will have to decide how much is returnable if this cannot be agreed.

PROFITS MADE AFTER DISSOLUTION

An account of partnership dealings must be kept following the dissolution of the partnership, because the winding-up period may sometimes be protracted. The general rule is that profits made after dissolution are shared between partners in the normal, profit-sharing ratio.

The 1890 Act provides that, where dissolution is triggered by the death of a partner or a partner otherwise ceasing to be a member of the firm, the court has a discretion to pay to the outgoing partner (or to his estate) such share of post-dissolution profits as may be considered to be attributable to the use of the former partner's share of the partnership assets. As usual, this provision is subject to contrary agreement and, judging by the case law, it is best to avoid the process of deciding how far profits are attributable to the use of the absent person's assets, and how far they are attributable to the goodwill and acumen of the remaining partners.

Where the continuing partners have an option to acquire the former partner's share of the assets (which will be quite usual in a partnership agreement) then, provided the terms of the option are complied with, the former partner's right to a share of the profits is excluded.

DISTRIBUTION OF ASSETS AND ADJUSTMENT OF ACCOUNTS

On dissolution, partnership accounts must be prepared, incorporating any final adjustments required to reflect the rights and obligations of the individual partners. If there is a partnership agreement, it will be necessary to consult it closely at this stage.

Subject to any such agreement, the 1890 Act provides as follows.

(1) Losses are to be dealt with first. These should be met as far as possible out of profits, then out of capital and finally, if necessary, by partners individually in the proportion in which they were previously entitled to share profits.

(2) the firm's assets, including sums contributed by the partners to make up losses or deficiencies of capital, will be applied as follows:

 – in paying the debts and liabilities of the firm to outsiders; then
 – in paying to each partner proportionately what is due from the firm to him in respect of the capital he put in; then
 – in dividing anything that is left among the partners according to their profit-sharing ratio.

NOTICE OF DISSOLUTION

A general notice of dissolution will normally be given by advertisement. In addition, a specific notice should be sent to all existing clients or customers of the firm. This is important for the firm as a whole because the notice signifies termination of a partner's authority to bind the firm.

PARTNERS' RIGHTS AS TO APPLICATION OF PROPERTY

When a partnership is dissolved, any partner is entitled to insist that the firm's assets are applied, first, in meeting the firm's debts and liabilities and, subsequently (if there is a surplus), in paying to each partner his agreed share. The idea here is that partnership assets are kept for partnership creditors, and are not available for the creditors of an individual partner. As we have seen (see p 19) this arrangement is usually known as a partner's 'lien' and any partner is entitled to enforce it by asking the court to order a sale of the assets.

DEATH OF A PARTNER

As we have already noted, the 1890 Act provides that the death of a partner will dissolve the relationship between *all* partners, unless there is agreement to the contrary. The consequences of a general dissolution will usually be highly inconvenient and intended partners should seek to ensure that the partnership agreement provides that only the relationship between the deceased and his fellow partners shall come to an end and that the relationship between the surviving partners should continue. In addition, it is sensible to provide for an appropriate method of valuing a deceased partner's share in the business.

The role of the personal representatives

'Personal representatives' is a generic term which includes *executors*, who derive their authority from a valid will and *administrators* who are appointed by the court where an individual dies intestate or leaves only an incomplete or invalid will.

Whatever the name, the job of the personal representative is to step into the shoes of the person who has died, collect in his assets, pay his outstanding debts and distribute his estate to those entitled to inherit it.

When dealing with the estate of a former partner, personal representatives are in a difficult position. They have no general legal power to carry on the business in their representative capacity and, if they do get involved, they run the risk of being held out as partners and, consequently, of incurring personal liability for the firm's debts. One of their main concerns will be to realise the value of the deceased partner's share in the firm's assets for the beneficiaries of the deceased partner's estate. In addition, the personal representatives may have to contemplate suing the firm in respect of any profits due to the deceased partner and not accounted for and, indeed, they themselves may be subject to proceedings by the continuing partners in respect of debts incurred by the deceased partner up to the date of death.

The legal duty of the personal representatives is a fiduciary one, and is owed to the beneficiaries of the deceased partner's estate. It will be apparent, therefore, that a continuing partner who is appointed personal representative may find himself in a difficult position and may face a conflict of interest.

The continuing partners

The death of a partner may embarrass a firm financially, even where provision has been made in the partnership agreement for business to continue. The deceased partner's personal representatives are obliged to realise his assets as quickly as possible and, in addition, the remaining partners may feel a strong moral obligation to allow provision to be made for his widow and dependent children without too much delay.

Financial problems may be eased if partners effect suitable insurance cover and if all partners agree, when making their separate wills, expressly to allow their personal representatives increased flexibility in the administration of their estates. If partners are to be personal representatives for each other then it would be helpful to include in individual wills, provisions which address any potential conflict of interest which may arise. In particular, a partner acting as personal representative must be empowered to conclude agreements with the firm which could not subsequently be set aside because of his personal interest.

Finally, it is sensible to provide in the partnership agreement procedures which will allow continuing partners to purchase the share of the deceased partner from his personal representatives. This will usually be the most satisfactory financial outcome for the continuing partners and also for the beneficiaries of the estate.

CHAPTER 9
Insolvency ★★★

INTRODUCTION

Insolvency is the inability to pay debts. Insolvency may affect a partnership in two ways.

(1) First, the firm may be insolvent, with the consequence that the creditors, being unable to recover their debts out of the firm's assets, may seek to turn against the personal assets of individual partners.

(2) Alternatively, one partner may be unable to meet his individual liabilities arising outside the firm, so that his creditors are anxious to obtain his share of the partnership assets in order to satisfy their debts.

The law of insolvency was substantially updated and consolidated by the Insolvency Act 1986 and, for the most part, the law is now appropriately adapted for today's business world. In the process of change, however, partnership insolvency law, unfortunately, became one of the more complex areas of the new system. Details of the procedures lie outside the scope of this book, and any firm facing financial difficulties would be wise to seek expert advice sooner rather than later. The following represents only a brief outline of the present law on insolvent partnerships.

LIMITED COMPANY PROCEDURES

Before 1986, partnerships were subjected to individual bankruptcy procedures, a reflection of the fact that, legally, a firm is only a collection of individual partners and has no separate corporate status. So, a bankruptcy receiving order could be made against the firm and would operate as if it had been made against each partner individually. A trustee in bankruptcy would be appointed to rationalise the debts and administer the assets, according to the law.

The main change brought about by the Insolvency Act 1986 is that, where the firm itself is insolvent, it will now be wound up by the companies court, in the same way that a limited company would be wound up, and not under individual bankruptcy procedures. In addition, where individual insolvency proceedings are brought against two or more members of an insolvent firm, who are also themselves personally insolvent, these too must be launched in the companies court. In these cases, the court must hear the petition against the firm first, and will only be required to make orders against individual partners if the debt remains unpaid.

An important consequence of using the limited company procedure is that partners will be regarded as equivalent to company directors, and will be subjected to the same sanctions which are applied under the Insolvency Act 1986 to directors who engage in *wrongful* or *fraudulent* trading.

This means that, if it is shown that the partner has engaged in fraudulent or wrongful trading, the court has power to make a disqualification order against him to prevent him becoming a member of any other partnership during a prescribed period. Wrongful trading occurs where a partner continues to carry on business in the knowledge that the firm is insolvent; fraudulent trading occurs where the partner carries on business with the intention to defraud the firm's creditors.

INDIVIDUAL BANKRUPTCY PROCEEDINGS

The alternative to using the companies court procedures is for creditors to bring bankruptcy proceedings against individual partners. This could involve the trustees of the partners' assets winding up the partnership business, although not as an unregistered company. The option is not available if the firm has a corporate partner. It is also possible to bring individual proceedings against one or more partners without involving the other partners and without winding up the firm.

NEW PROPOSALS

The Insolvency Act 1986 introduced simpler and cheaper alternatives to formal winding up for insolvent companies. These are as follows.

(1) A voluntary arrangement procedure allowing a company to enter into an agreement with its creditors providing for a moratorium on repayment of debts or repayment of less than the full amount due in full settlement. Shareholders must approve the agreement.

(2) Administration orders, which may be made by the court to rescue companies which have a chance of survival or to produce a more advantageous realisation of the company's assets than would be achieved on a winding-up.

Up to now, these procedures have not been available to insolvent partnerships, but the Department of Trade and Industry is currently reviewing the position and, at the time of writing, it proposes to harmonise the rules so that partnerships are put in substantially the same position as limited companies, subject only to the fact that the individual bankruptcy rules will continue to apply to partnerships alongside the corporate procedures.

THE INSOLVENCY PRACTITIONER

Before 1986 there was no legal requirement for an accountant, business adviser or other person to have any formal qualification in order to deal with the complicated procedures which operate when there is an insolvency. The Insolvency Act 1986 removed this weakness in the law, and introduced a new title for such people, that of insolvency practitioner. Only licensed insolvency practitioners are now permitted to deal with insolvent companies or with the affairs of an insolvent partnership.

The change was necessary to ensure that advisers in insolvency matters have the required experience, knowledge and professionalism to perform their duties to the highest standard. It is now an offence for an unlicensed person to deal with insolvency matters.

APPLICATION OF ASSETS ON AN INSOLVENCY

As explained in Chapter 5, each partner is jointly liable to a creditor for debts and obligations incurred whilst he was a partner in the firm. When a firm is dissolved, each partner is entitled, against the other partners, to have the partnership assets applied in payment of the firm's debts and liabilities. If such assets are insufficient, the partners must make up the deficiency in the proportions in which they were entitled to share profits.

Where a firm becomes insolvent, however, the partners are likely to become personally insolvent too, because their own private property may be insufficient to meet their share of the partnership losses as well as their own private debts. In these circumstances the rule is that the firm's assets must be treated as the primary source for payment of the firm's debts, whilst the assets of individual partners remain the primary source for payment of their individual debts. Only if there is a surplus in one source can that surplus be used to pay the debts primarily payable out of the other source. So, in the bankruptcy of an individual partner, his private creditors will take priority over the claims of creditors of the firm.

This rule does not fully reflect the general principles on which the liability of partners is based, and it has been subjected to much criticism over the years. In particular, it is seen as being unfair to a firm's creditors to prevent them from receiving dividends from an individual partner's property until all his personal creditors have been paid in full.

The Department of Trade and Industry is now recommending that the law be changed so that joint creditors of the firm should compete equally with partners' individual creditors for payment out of partners' separate estates.

In addition, not all creditors are equal. The Inland Revenue, for instance, ranks in priority to other creditors, as does HM Customs and Excise in respect of VAT. Secured creditors – for example, mortgagees who hold a charge over the firm's assets to secure their debts – will also take priority by relying on their security.

CHAPTER 10
Using Professionals

INTRODUCTION

No business can expect to be successful without taking some sort of professional advice whenever this becomes necessary. Different partnerships will be run by individuals with expertise in their own specialist areas. Should the occasion arise when they feel they are in need of assistance in an area which is unfamiliar to them, they should seek help and advice from a specialist in that particular field, just as their own clients or customers will do from them. So, an architect encountering a problem of construction law will probably seek the advice of a solicitor, and a dentist wishing to prepare his accounts would be well-advised to engage an accountant.

EMPLOYING A PROFESSIONAL IS ECONOMICAL

Since time is money it makes no sense to embark on a voyage of discovery, but it makes good sense to adopt the principle of 'horses for courses'. The value of qualified professional advice should, therefore, be only too apparent to firms whose partners have themselves undertaken a long and arduous professional training, and the fact that the majority of professionals are authorised and controlled by their own governing bodies, and carry professional insurance, is an added safeguard.

FEES

Accountants, solicitors and other professionals are frequently regarded as being expensive in terms of the service which they provide. But the 'opportunity cost' of a partner engaging in any activity which is not directly profit-related must be weighed very carefully. Many hours can be spent, fruitlessly, in trying to solve an extraneous problem, when the cost of employing a professional would be far less than the cost of the lost time. If a client does feel that he has been charged excessively for work which has been carried out he should raise this point with his adviser and request a breakdown of the costs and expenses incurred. The best advice, however, is to negotiate the professional fee before, not after, advice is given.

TYPES OF PROFESSIONAL ADVISERS

There are many types of professional advisers – surveyors and valuers, architects, solicitors, accountants, actuaries (who deal with pension funds and investments), patent and copyright experts, marketing and advertising specialists, computer consultants, insurance brokers, and many more – but a new business is most likely to need advice from an accountant, a solicitor or a bank manager.

CHOOSING ADVISERS

Accountants

Accountants offer a wide range of financial advice, which is not confined to business accounts. They practise either alone as sole practitioners, or in a partnership. There is now no limit on the number of partners per firm, and some firms are very large. As a general rule, the large firms will offer a wider range of professional services than smaller firms, and will probably charge more. There are different types of qualification in accountancy but, generally speaking, those who trade as firms and offer their services to the public, are chartered accountants.

WHAT SHOULD AN ACCOUNTANT DO FOR THE FIRM?

The areas in which an accountant's skills will be of assistance to a firm include the following.

(1) Discussing the start-up of the business, and assisting with forecasts and projections.

(2) Providing help and advice in the raising of suitable finance.

(3) Organising an accounting and management information system for the firm.

(4) Advising on partnership taxation.

(5) Advising on VAT.

(6) Advising on payroll, PAYE and National Insurance systems, and the employment of staff generally.

(7) Providing ongoing business advice as the business starts to trade and to expand.

(8) Providing tax planning advice at periodic intervals.

(9) Discussing computerisation, suggesting suitable software and hardware and outlining necessary controls to include in the accounting system.

(10) Preparing partnership accounts and discussing taxation and other matters arising from the accounts.

(11) Acting as a 'sounding board' for ideas and potential projects as they arise.

(12) Advising on action required in the event of business difficulties and recommending an appropriate course of action, for example recommending consulting a licensed insolvency practitioner.

HOW SHOULD A FIRM CHOOSE AN ACCOUNTANT?

The best way to choose an accountant, if the firm has no one particularly in mind, is for it to seek a recommendation. This could be from a business colleague who is satisfied with the services that he is receiving from his accountant or, failing that, from the firm's solicitor or bank manager who will know of a good local firm with the knowledge and experience to be able to provide sound and up-to-date advice. It makes good sense, at least in the early stages of a business, that the firm uses the same firm of accountants for all the services required in order to facilitate a good professional relationship based on knowledge of all aspects of the firm's business.

Auditors

Whilst partnerships are not subject to the detailed accounting rules which affect limited companies under the companies legislation, in practice, at least where a firm is of a substantial size, an annual audit will be carried out. Most accountancy firms will provide this service.

Solicitors

A firm's need for a solicitor will vary depending on what kind of business it is in, but there are several areas where legal advice is likely to be needed.

(1) Drafting the partnership agreement – probably the most important task of all.

(2) Providing help and advice in the raising of finance.

(3) Advising on individual estate planning for partners. This would include preparing wills and advising on capital gains tax and inheritance tax.

(4) Advising on protection of 'intellectual property', such as trade or service marks, copyright, patents, and designs.

(5) Dealing with matters relating to credit control, debt collection and other litigation.

(6) Dealing with the leasing or purchasing of partnership property.

(7) Advising on regulatory and compliance requirements as to, for example, the giving of credit, and on requirements relating to obtaining licences to carry on certain businesses.

(8) Advising on professional negligence.

(9) Advising on employment-related matters such as redundancy, unfair or wrongful dismissal, maternity rights, health and safety and discrimination on the basis of race or gender.

(10) Drafting standard business contracts.

(11) Advising on supply contracts, such as contracts to acquire computer systems.

(12) Advising on the action required in the event of a partnership dispute or the firm getting into financial difficulties.

(13) Dealing with incorporation of the partnership if and when this becomes commercially desirable.

It is worth noting that there is an overlap between the professional services offered by accountants and by solicitors, and when the firm needs both it is useful if they can work well together. Once again, choosing a solicitor will very often be the result of a recommendation and, as with accountancy, larger firms will offer a wider range of specialised services and their fees will be higher. With solicitors, however, a firm should not assume that all firms of solicitors will offer general business advice, since there is probably more specialisation amongst solicitors than amongst accountants. Many solicitors, for instance, deal mainly with non-commercial matters, such as crime or matrimonial disputes, and may not have the necessary expertise to provide all-round business advice, particularly to a large partnership.

Bank managers

In many cases, the first approach to a bank will be in order to obtain funding for a business. It is essential that any request for borrowing is presented in a correct and professional manner, as a bank will be influenced in its decision not only by the commercial sense of a project but also by its assessment of the people involved in the project, and the quality and professionalism of the presentation.

For this reason, if funding of any substance is being sought from a bank, it will be necessary to prepare a business plan, which is a summary of the proposed project, together with cash flow forecasts and projected accounts. The firm's financial advisers should have experience in this field, and will be able to assist not only in the preparation of the business plan but also in the presentation of the plan to the bank.

Bank managers are, generally, very experienced in assessing situations and appraising the potential success of business projects. They will not normally lend in high-risk situations, or without adequate security to support borrowing. They also have wide knowledge of business and will be a useful source of advice on many financial matters.

CHAPTER 11
Other Considerations

FINANCING THE PARTNERSHIP ★

We have seen from Chapter 1 that a partnership is essentially a relationship between individuals who are engaged in a common business venture with the aim of making a profit. The Partnership Act 1890 ('the 1890 Act') goes no further than this in terms of a definition, so that the law itself makes no distinction between a partner who devotes all his energies to working for the firm and a partner who turns up at the office occasionally and spends the rest of his time on the golf course. Again, the law does not require capital contributions, common management, common assets, common facilities, a common bank account or a common firm name, although all these things would conventionally be associated with the notion of partnership. But all partners are equally liable to the outside world; and they will share equally the profits and losses of the firm, subject only to the internal arrangements laid down in any partnership agreement.

The law does not, of course, require a partnership agreement before it will regard individuals as partners, and this is why lending money to a firm may not be an entirely straightforward business. In practice, there may be a fine line between putting up finance and becoming a creditor of the firm and being a token or sleeping partner. At one time the courts always accepted that any creditor who was to be repaid out of the firm's profits was automatically to be regarded as a partner. Now the 1890 Act states that the repayment of a loan out of profits or the payment of interest on a loan out of profits will not automatically make the lender a partner. It is clear, however, that the very existence of such an arrangement may still raise that inference and, consequently, someone who only intends to finance a business and not become a partner in it needs to make sure that the financial arrangement is clearly expressed and properly documented. It remains the case that any agreement whereby a 'lender' agrees to share the risk of loss as well as profits will almost inevitably make him a partner.

The following points may be worth bearing in mind on both sides when a financing arrangement is being negotiated.

(1) The payment made must be a true loan, not a contribution to a joint venture. A lender can expect to have no voice in the management of the business and no right to prevent its assets from being squandered or misused. The lender's entitlement is simply to claim repayment from the borrower, and there must be a personal liability on the part of the borrower to repay it.

(2) The lender must not take an interest in, or share of, the capital of the firm. Nor must his share of the profits (if that is the specified mode of repayment) depend upon the relationship between his loan and the remainder of the firm's capital.

(3) Reference to words or phrases which are usually found in partnership agreements should be avoided. For example, loan agreements should not contain terms like 'capital'; 'partnership'; 'venture'.

(4) Equally, loan agreements should not be excessively technical and should not, if possible, include clauses which are closely associated with partnership agreements.

LIMITED PARTNERSHIPS

Limited partnerships are hybrids. An individual may limit his liability, and take on a role which resembles that of a shareholder in a limited company, but the firm itself does not, in any sense, acquire separate legal personality. Limited partnerships always remain combinations of individuals carrying on a particular profession or business.

The operative legislation dates from 1907, and is little used in practice, mainly because many of its provisions reflect the companies legislation without offering, in most cases, a viable alternative to incorporation. In particular, there are tight registration requirements which make the constitution of a limited partnership common knowledge, and also impose a burden of compliance which does not affect ordinary partnerships.

Legally speaking, the Limited Partnership Act 1907 ('the 1907 Act') acts as a gloss on the rest of partnership law. There are two main differences between limited and ordinary partnerships.

(1) Formation

As with private companies and European Economic Interest Groupings, a limited partnership is set up by a prescribed administrative procedure. As has been noted, however, registration makes the firm's constitution public knowledge; *it does not provide incorporation.*

(2) **Internal structure**

Limited partnerships lack three of the essential characteristics of an ordinary partnership, which are:

- the unlimited liability of every partner;

- the implied authority of every partner to bind the firm in any transaction within the ordinary scope of the partnership business (see Chapter 5); and

- the right of each partner to take part in management of the business.

A limited partner is defined as someone who contributes a fixed amount of capital to the firm, and whose liability is limited to that sum. In other words, his personal estate is not under threat if the firm goes to the wall. The registration requirements mentioned above are clearly intended to give potential creditors notice of this fact. Companies may be limited partners and, indeed, most limited partnerships encountered nowadays are joint venture arrangements between limited companies. It is important to note, however, that not all partners are permitted to limit their liability in this way. The 1907 Act states that a limited partnership must have at least one general partner, who carries unlimited liability for all debts and obligations of the firm.

The price of limited liability is the fact that limited partners are expected only to invest capital and to leave the running of the business to others. The 1907 Act forbids a limited partner to take part, either directly or indirectly, in the management of the firm. If he dabbles he will forfeit his protection from the outside world.

In practice, this is the major reason why limited partnerships have not become popular. In most small enterprises, incorporated or not, it is unrealistic to separate investment from management. The law creates artificial boundaries, in order to balance the interests of partners and creditors, but the model which has been created clearly does not meet the needs of business people sufficiently accurately to provide a viable alternative to incorporation. Even professional partnerships, which cannot incorporate, have not been persuaded that the limited partnership model has anything to offer them.

SALARIED PARTNERS *

The expression 'salaried partner' is, to some extent, a contradiction in terms. A salaried partner is, essentially, an employee who is held out as a partner. In many professional firms the status is seen as a stepping-stone in career development terms, between employee and full, equity partner. In many respects, however, the status is an unenviable one. Whilst, at one level, it is a measure of professional success, salaried partners in fact find themselves taking on the financial risks of partnership, without necessarily enjoying the compensating privileges.

In a solicitors' firm, for example, salaried partners enjoy a higher status than assistant (ie employed) solicitors but, by definition, they are not profit sharing. Their remuneration will consist of a fixed salary, which may or may not be linked to profitability. They will not make capital contributions to the firm, nor will they participate fully in management. They may, for instance, be invited to partners' meetings, but are unlikely to have a right to vote. They are also unlikely to have access to all the information that is available to equity partners. They will be taxed as employees, without the benefit of the preceding year basis of assessment (see p 57).

On the other hand, the outside world draws no distinction between salaried and equity partners. The addition of a new name to the firm's notepaper carries with it a representation of partnership, which means joint and several liability for the obligations of the firm. In practice, although equity partners do tend to shoulder the smaller financial burdens, if the firm runs into real difficulties, and becomes insolvent, *all* partners, salaried partners included, will be liable for its debts.

EMPLOYEES

Partners cannot be employees. Partners, collectively, are the owners of a business and because the firm itself does not have separate legal status they, as individuals, are also employers. Employers cannot employ themselves. This explains why the concept of salaried partner is really a contradiction in terms. In a small limited company, on the other hand, a sole director may be employed in the company's business. Firms will obviously wish to employ people who are not owners of the business, and the hiring and firing of staff will always be within the ostensible authority of a partner, even if not expressly referred to in the partnership agreement itself.

The legal distinction between partner and employee is very important. A partner will be self-employed and taxed as such under Schedule D; his position in the firm will be governed by general partnership law as expressed in the Partnership Act 1890 and, more importantly, by the terms of his firm's own partnership agreement. He will have no statutory protection against dismissal or redundancy. An employee will be taxed under Schedule E; his position will be governed by a contract with his employer but, in addition, he will be entitled to the protection of the general law in relation to such questions as redundancy; unfair or wrongful dismissal and equal pay.

Employment law is complex and partners, as employers, will be well advised to seek professional advice if things go wrong. The traditional power of the employer to hire and fire staff and to set the conditions of work is now considerably overlaid by complex statutory protection for employees and no firm will wish to run the risk of damaging its business by falling foul of these provisions. The aim of this section will be to highlight some of the most important concerns for partners who employ staff.

The contract of employment ★★

The contract of employment is the basis of the employment relationship. No particular legal requirements are attached to its drafting or presentation, although a written contract is likely to minimise later disagreements. Under the Employment Protection Consolidation Act 1978, however, full-time employees are entitled to a written statement of the main terms of their contract. This is usually referred to as the statement of 'Terms and Conditions of Employment'.

When preparing contracts of employment professional partnerships may need to pay particular attention to restraint or anti-competition clauses, and here legal advice will often be needed. In practice, however, the many statutory rights and obligations imposed by law on a contract of employment are as important as the terms expressed by the parties, and they may not be waived despite any attempt, by either side, to override them.

The following are perhaps the most important statutory rights of employees:

- not to be discriminated against on grounds of race, sex or marriage;

- equal pay with members of the opposite sex if it can be shown that they are doing like work or work of equal value;

- an itemised pay statement;

- maternity benefits;

- redundancy pay;

- a safe system of work;

- statutory sick pay;

- protected employment rights on the transfer of a business;

- not to be unfairly dismissed.

It is worth noting that some of these rights are subject to qualifying periods of service.

Health and safety ★★

Compliance with health and safety legislation must now be a major concern for all employers. Since the implementation of the Health & Safety at Work Act 1974, all employers have been obliged to:

- provide and maintain a safe working environment and safe systems of work;
- make arrangements to ensure safety and the absence of health risks connected with the use, handling, storage and transport of articles and substances;
- provide information, instruction, training and supervision to ensure the health and safety of employees;
- provide and maintain a safe working environment free from health risks and also provide adequate welfare facilities.

A firm with five or more employees must prepare a written statement of its health and safety policy and bring this to the notice of all employees.

Beyond this, 1993 has been a year of further change for UK health and safety law. European Community legislation aimed at harmonising and strengthening health and safety standards across the Community has now been implemented in the UK by various sets of Regulations which came into force on 1 January 1993. These apply to all businesses, irrespective of size, and require employers, for example:

- to assess risks in their own working environment and identify protective or preventive measures to minimise them;
- to ensure that suitable equipment, proper maintenance, training, information and instruction is provided for employees. In particular, there is a set of Regulations on the use of VDU equipment which has not previously been covered by specific legislation.

Most of the new Regulations simply add to the basic obligations under the 1974 Act and promote 'best practice' but, at the same time, compliance will involve additional burdens of administration and cost.

Insurance

Employers must insure all employees against liability for injury and disease suffered in the course of, or because of, their employment. Employers should also consider insuring against the following risks:

- public liability;
- fire and special perils;
- theft;
- business interruption;
- documents and goods in transit;

- personal accident;

- personal health.

As has been mentioned elsewhere (see page 28), professional indemnity cover will be compulsory for many firms.

ACQUISITIONS AND AMALGAMATIONS ★★

In today's competitive market-place, professional firms may see expansion as an answer to increasing overheads and diminishing profit margins.

Firms may choose to expand generically, by taking on new staff or opening new branch offices. Alternatively, they may look towards taking over or amalgamating with other firms with which they may previously have been in competition. From a strategic point of view such a venture may enable firms to combine their strengths and seek to eliminate their weaknesses.

It is clear, however, that many amalgamations are unsuccessful. This is usually because firms seeking this method of expansion sometimes fail adequately to address underlying cultural differences between them. Pre-merger negotiations should therefore be exhaustive, and the following issues will be particularly important: the name of the new firm; the hierarchy of partners; the composition and powers of the management team; the location of the new firm; financial arrangements for partners, and the new business objective. In principle, it is essential that a new partnership agreement be prepared for the merged firm.

As a matter of law the reconstitution of a firm through a merger or amalgamation is likely to be subject to the continuity of employment rules under the Transfer of Undertakings (Protection of Employment) Regulations 1981. This means that all contracts of employment will have effect as though the partners in the newly constituted firm were the original employers, and all employment protection rights will be preserved. Dismissal of an employee simply because of the transfer of the business will automatically be unfair. In addition, in some circumstances, a merger or acquisition may be a breach of competition law. Under the Fair Trading Act 1973 where two or more enterprises 'cease to be distinct' and, in so doing, acquire a combined market share of 25 per cent or more in relation to a substantial part of the UK, there may be a reference to the Monopolies and Mergers Commission. The House of Lords recently held that South Yorkshire, together with parts of Nottinghamshire, was appropriately 'substantial'. Finally, the Restrictive Trade Practices Act 1975 may apply to an agreement between two firms (whether or not made in context of a merger) which purports to inhibit the operation of a free market in relation to goods or services.

CHAPTER 12

To Incorporate or Not? ★★★

INTRODUCTION

At some time or another most businesses have to balance the benefits of incorporation as a limited company against the benefits of partnership (or of operating as a sole trader). Sometimes this decision will be made on start-up of the business. Frequently, however, a business will begin its life as an individual enterprise or a small partnership and, later on, with expansion, will consider incorporation.

Professional partnerships are not necessarily immune from this consideration. Before 'Big Bang' in 1986 many stockbroking businesses were incorporated and sold to banks and other financial institutions. In the past few years estate agents and surveyors, formerly practising in partnership, have transferred their businesses to companies, and these in turn have been taken over by the financial sector. The prohibition on incorporation by firms of solicitors has recently been lifted, and chartered accountants and architects are similarly placed. Doctors may now incorporate themselves, but dentists and veterinary surgeons are still not permitted to limit their liability.

The arguments for and against incorporation fall under the following headings:

- liability;
- formality;
- status;
- management;
- taxation.

LIABILITY

As we have seen, all partners are liable *without limit* for all the debts of a partnership. Each partner stands to lose not only what he has invested in the business but also any other property which he owns. Although partners can agree between themselves, through the partnership agreement, how losses are to be shared between them, this will not prevent a creditor pursuing his debt in full against a partner.

A company, on the other hand, is usually said to have limited liability. This is not strictly true. In fact it is the liability of the shareholders which is limited, and this is because the company is a separate legal person carrying on a business, and is not identified with its shareholders. A company's liability for the debts of its business is unlimited, in the same way as any other individual's would be, and, by the same token, an under-capitalised company is like an impecunious individual – a bad business risk. A shareholder's obligation, however, is only to pay for his shares in full. Beyond that he has no liability to meet the company's debts, and consequently he is in a very different position from a partner in a firm.

There are obvious attractions for the small business in acquiring limited liability, but it will be apparent too that there are risks for customers or clients dealing with small companies, especially those which are commercially not very successful. It is precisely for this reason that a speculative business is most likely to be carried on by a company.

In practice, however, a number of factors will diminish the advantages of limited liability.

(1) Those who give credit to limited companies often require the directors or shareholders to give personal guarantees, which make them personally responsible for the company's debts should the company be unable to meet them. Sometimes, too, a director or shareholder will be asked to give a mortgage over his home, which means that if the company is failing to satisfy its creditors, the house may be sold to raise capital.

(2) Company directors who have acted fraudulently or in a way defined as improper by the companies' legislation may be made personally responsible for paying the company's debts; they will then be in the same position as partners.

(3) There may not be any real risk that the company's capital will be insufficient to meet its debts. For example, where the business consists in the provision of a service which does not entail large capital expenditure the main business problem is more likely to be getting in money which is owed to the company by others.

(4) Limited liability will not be of great advantage if the shareholder has already invested all his assets in the business.

FORMALITY

For a company, the price of limited liability is regulation, coupled with publicity. The following are some of the requirements that affect all limited companies.

(1) The companies' legislation lays down detailed requirements for the formation of a company and for its management structure. As well as adopting a memorandum and articles of association, a company is required to have at least one director and a secretary.

(2) Companies are required to prepare annual accounts and have them audited (certified) by an independent accountant.

(3) Companies are required to file numerous details with the Registrar of Companies – for example an annual return, particulars of directors, and changes in directors or the address of the registered office. The preparation of these documents adds to a company's running costs and is likely to mean that a large company will need to employ a company secretary or take regular advice from a solicitor or accountant.

(4) Companies are required to make their records, including their annual accounts, available for public inspection. The purpose of this rule is to allow those who deal with companies to satisfy themselves as to a company's commercial standing. No such requirements affect partnerships, which may keep their financial position secret, although in practice, prospective lenders are likely to want to see the firm's accounts.

All these requirements add to the cost of setting up and running a limited company, and whilst the cost of a well-drafted partnership agreement may also be substantial, it is probably fair to say that the running costs of a company are considerably in excess of those of a partnership.

STATUS

Although many large and reputable businesses are carried on by sole traders or partners, the public assumes, rightly or wrongly, that a company has more financial credibility than an unincorporated firm.

This is reflected in the fact that a company can often raise new money, by borrowing, more readily than a partnership can. As a general rule, for example, banks will be more prepared to lend money to companies than to sole traders or partners. A company's scope for borrowing is also enhanced by its power to create a special sort of mortgage over its property, called a *floating charge*, as a security for money it borrows. A partnership cannot do this.

Apart from borrowing, a company can also raise capital by issuing new shares, whereas a partnership would have to introduce a new partner to the business in order to provide new capital. It is likely that a prospective investor would be far more cautious about the prospect of acquiring joint and several unlimited liability as a partner in a firm than he would be about buying shares in a company and taking the protection of limited liability.

MANAGEMENT

A shareholder can control a company which is carrying on a business and receive dividends if the company's business makes a profit, without having to become involved in the day-to-day running of the business. The same is not usually true of a sole trader or partners. For example, partners carrying on a business know that they will have to pay the debts of the business if things go wrong, so they will naturally be reluctant to entrust the management of the business to someone else. Even if the size of the business requires the appointment of managers, the partners will probably take an active interest on a day-to-day basis. As has been pointed out (see p 13) the identification of ownership and management may result in inefficiency in a partnership, and may make it uncompetitive in the market-place.

Shareholders, on the other hand, having the protection of limited liability, are more likely to permit their company business to be managed by others without feeling the need to intervene unduly. Company law provides that shareholders have power to appoint (and remove) directors, whose job it is to manage the business of the company. The law puts directors in a position of trust in looking after the company's business, and they are subject to all sorts of duties and liabilities, often quite onerous. By this means the shareholders and the company itself are given protection against abuse of their position by the directors. From a management point of view the delegation of authority to directors has many attractions and, indeed, the largest professional partnerships (for example some accountants and solicitors) tend to adopt, by agreement, a corporate management structure, notwithstanding the unlimited liability of partners.

TAXATION

Partnership taxation is considered in more detail in Chapter 7. A brief summary may be useful, however, in the context of the present discussion.

Where a business is carried on by a sole trader he pays income tax on profits and capital gains tax on capital gains. The rule is the same for partnerships, except that the partners' profits and gains are amalgamated and charged to income tax and capital gains tax in a joint assessment. Where a company carries on business, however, it pays only one tax – corporation tax – on both profits and gains.

Rates of tax are different, although these differences are slowly being eroded. In addition, the profits and gains which are subject to tax are worked out differently, and the taxes are assessed and become payable at different times.

In general, a partnership offers less scope for tax planning in relation to income profits than a limited company, because all profits are taxed as the partners' income, whether they are actually drawn or retained in the business. On the other hand, at the moment, the preceding year basis of assessment gives partnerships a cash flow advantage.

For companies the taxation of profits will depend on whether those profits are distributed as dividends, or as directors' fees, or whether they are retained in the business. Retained profits will attract corporation tax at a rate of between 25 per cent and 33 per cent, depending on the size of the company. Profits which are distributed as directors' fees will be subject to income tax at the appropriate rate for those to whom they are paid, but sums paid out as dividends will be treated as part of the company's taxable profits, and so will bear corporation tax.

As far as capital gains are concerned, the maximum rate of corporation tax payable by a company is 33 per cent, which contrasts with the 40 per cent capital gains tax payable by a partner. On the other hand, more general exemptions and reliefs are available to partners than to companies.

It is difficult to generalise on the respective fiscal advantages and disadvantages of partnerships as opposed to limited companies, but where profits are small it is probably true to say that there is no clear advantage either way.

The more profitable a business becomes, however, the more likely it is that the corporation tax rules will produce a lower tax bill than the income and capital gains tax rules. That is why a business usually begins by being owned by a sole trader or partners but is subsequently transferred to a company, formed for that purpose, at a financially appropriate moment. One factor which lends itself to this particular sequence of events is that a loss made in the first three years of a new partnership business can be carried back and set off against income of the partners in the three years before the business was set up. A person who sets up a company is not entitled to any such relief.

PENSIONS AND NATIONAL INSURANCE

With regard to pensions and National Insurance it is important to note that company directors and partners are treated differently, and that partners are at a disadvantage in respect of pension provisions. Directors can take advantage of 'exempt approved pension schemes' which give substantial tax relief on contributions by both employers and employees, and provide further relief on capital taxes to the scheme managers. Such schemes provide pensions and, in many cases, lump sums on retirement. They are not available to the self-employed nor, consequently, to partners.

The social security system also operates differently in respect of employees and the self-employed. National Insurance contributions by a company and its directors are significantly greater than contributions payable by a self-employed person, such as a partner. However, the benefits to which an employed person is entitled are correspondingly higher than those which can be claimed by someone who is self-employed.

CONCLUSIONS

Clearly, various factors will influence the decision whether or not to incorporate, always assuming that the law allows a particular enterprise to limit its liability.

In many cases, the desirability of limited liability may outweigh other considerations. However, as has been seen, limited liability will make little difference where the shareholders have put everything they own into the business. Generally speaking, limited liability will be most important where there is a substantial risk of loss of capital, and the prospective shareholders have private wealth which will not be invested in the business. Where limited liability is not the main criterion, tax factors may be more significant, and will need to be evaluated carefully.

In addition the administrative rules which affect companies, plus the costs of compliance, need to be considered carefully, especially in the case of small businesses. It is worth noting here that one result of UK membership of the European Community has been that the attractiveness of the small private company as a vehicle for carrying on business has been enhanced. Ten years ago, company law generally started to become increasingly interventionist, in the public interest, and there was a very real prospect that small companies would be swamped by the statutory requirements. At that point it looked as though partnership might once again become the preferred medium for a small business. In many European countries, however, there is a far greater legal distinction between public (ie quoted on the stock exchange) and private companies than there has been in the UK, and recent European inspired legislation has had the effect of widening the distinction in English law too. One visible effect of this is the use of the ending 'PLC' rather than 'Ltd' on a public company's name. In particular, small companies are excluded from some of the new and stringent accounting disclosure rules, and small companies and private companies are also now permitted to dispense with certain internal procedures, such as the holding of an annual general meeting. These changes mean that running costs for a private company are reduced and there are fewer procedural pitfalls to catch out the unwary directors.

In general, the conclusion has to be that the decision whether or not to incorporate will be, at least partly, subjective, but that once a business has grown to a certain size, and assuming that there are no legal constraints, then incorporation will become almost inevitable for financial and commercial reasons. The most difficult question may be to decide when the moment to incorporate has actually arrived, and here a firm will need to rely on skilled professional advice. Where incorporation is the outcome it may be useful to refer to the companion volume by D Impey and N Montague *Running a Limited Company* (Jordans, 1990) for further information regarding limited companies.

CHAPTER 13

Common Partnership Problems

In this final chapter, some of the problems which commonly afflict people in partnerships will be identified and briefly discussed. Cross-references to relevant sections of the text are provided, but the reader is once again reminded of the wisdom of seeking good professional advice at an early stage when things go wrong.

Q: Do you *have* to have a formal partnership agreement?

A: There is no legal requirement for an agreement at all, but new partnerships should always consider preparing one. The choice lies between a firm being self-regulating – which follows to a large extent from the adoption of an agreement – or being regulated by general partnership law, which may or may not be satisfactory for the firm. Any agreement should be formal, in the sense that it is committed to writing.

Chapter 3 provides a checklist of possible heads of agreement, but it is always sensible to seek legal advice on the drafting in order to avert problems later on.

Q: How do you start up a partnership?

A: A partnership is a commercial venture set up by two or more people. There are no special formalities, as there are for setting up a limited company, and you can be treated as a partner – by the Inland Revenue for example – even if you have never thought about the legal nature of your relationship. It is always sensible to talk to your legal and financial advisers in advance about the appropriate medium for carrying on your particular profession or business. This is discussed further in Chapter 12.

Q: What is unlimited liability?

A: Partners in a firm are liable to outsiders for debts, obligations or wrongful acts committed or incurred by one of their number. If the liability is very considerable, the partners' own personal property may have to be made available to meet it.

Professional partnerships trade in their skill and judgment, and if mistakes are made claims are likely to be high. Consequently, most professional firms are required to carry suitable indemnity insurance cover.

The liability of partners is discussed further in Chapter 5.

Q: Should we think about limiting our liability?

A: In theory, you can limit your liability by incorporating your business as a limited company and being the directors of it. The company will be a legal person and will be liable to the extent of its assets just as an individual would be. This liability would not extend to the directors, although in practice they would need to give personal guarantees that they would meet certain obligations, particularly the repayment of business loans.

Professional firms may not be permitted to limit their liability through incorporation and you should always check on this. Otherwise you should consider whether the cost of incorporation, and the formalities involved, outweigh the disadvantages of unlimited liability.

These issues are discussed further in Chapter 12.

Q: I shall be retiring at the end of this year. Can I still be sued as a partner after that?

A: Technically speaking, once you cease to be a partner you can no longer be sued as such in respect of obligations incurred after the date of your retirement. This is subject to the proviso that you must ensure that notice of retirement is given to all clients of the firm and that your name is removed from the firm's notepaper. If you are aware now of any onerous potential liabilities it may be wise to try to negotiate an agreement with your partners that they will indemnify you against these. You cannot, however, avoid liability altogether for acts of the firm, or of any of your partners, prior to your retirement.

This point is discussed further at p 43.

Q: One of my partners is drinking a lot and has already upset some of our patients. How do we get rid of him?

A: If you have a partnership agreement which expressly provides for the expulsion of a partner from the firm, you can deal with this situation with the minimum of disruption. If not, then, unless your partner is prepared to acknowledge his condition and take early retirement, the only answer to your problem is dissolution of the firm. Most firms would face dissolution rather than retain a partner whose conduct is damaging to the firm's professional reputation but, in practice, it is much better if the partnership agreement contains an appropriately drafted expulsion clause.

Further discussion is to be found on p 75.

Q: My senior partner has committed the firm to the purchase of some expensive IT equipment, without consulting the rest of us. What can we do?

A: A supplier of equipment to the firm would be entitled to assume that your senior partner had authority to commit the firm. Any internal arrangements between partners about who should take major financial decisions will not affect outside creditors unless they are notified that only certain partners have authority to enter into agreements on behalf of the firm.

It is now up to you and your partners to prevent problems like this from arising again. If the situation is sufficiently serious you may consider invoking an expulsion clause in your partnership agreement, or even dissolving the firm. Otherwise it seems clear that there are some management issues which need to be thrashed out.

These issues are discussed further in Chapters 2 and 5.

Q: I am becoming increasingly unsettled in my firm because I can see opportunities for developing new business, but my partners will not support me. If I leave the firm to set up on my own, will there be any problems?

A: Your position depends on your partnership agreement. If there is a clause which prevents you from setting up in business in competition with your former partners then you will be bound by it unless you are able to challenge its validity on the basis that it is unreasonably in restraint of trade (see p 36). The outcome will depend on your type of business, your environment and on how the clause itself is drafted.

If, however, there is no relevant clause in your partnership agreement, you would not be subject to any implied restrictions on competition, even if you were to sell your goodwill in the firm to your former partners. You should resist pressure to enter into any express restraint agreement on your departure from the firm. You must not, however, solicit old customers or clients as long as they remain customers or clients of your old firm, nor must you represent yourself to the outside world as continuing the business of the firm.

Q: One of my partners is using the firm's client list to market a new business interest of his own. What is the legal position?

A: Assuming that the partnership as a whole has not approved this activity, it looks as though your partner is in breach of the general duty of good faith which arises out of the relationship between partners. This will be either because he has created a conflict of interest for himself by setting up a business which competes with the firm's business, or because he has simply used a partnership asset for his own ends. Either way, he must account to the firm for profits made and may be restrained by an injunction from continuing with these activities.

The fiduciary duties of partners are discussed further at p 11.

Q: One of my partners is showing early signs of dementia. He is forgetful, loses concentration easily and is often irritable. What can we do?

A: Partnership agreements usually provide that if a partner becomes a patient under the Mental Health Act 1983 his colleagues have the option of terminating their relationship with him.

The difficulty is that the partner may not recognise his own incapacity, and if he will not submit voluntarily to the Mental Health Act 1983 jurisdiction, compulsory powers will have to be invoked.

It is far better if the agreement contains a clause which permits the compulsory retirement of a partner who, for any reason, is unable to perform his obligations to the firm (see p 29). This point is particularly relevant where – as here – a partner's health may be subject to a very slow decline, and where he may not yet be incapable in the Mental Health Act 1983 sense.

If there is no partnership agreement, or no relevant clause, the partnership may be dissolved by the court on application by any partner (see p 75). The court will not order dissolution lightly, however, and will need to be convinced that there are no realistic prospects for recovery. This will mean relying on medical evidence which will be difficult to obtain without co-operation from the partner who is becoming incapable.

Q: One of my partners is an excellent after-dinner speaker, and often attends two or three functions a week during the dinner season. His reputation is such that he now commands quite substantial fees. Should he be asked to account to the firm for these?

A: A partner owes a duty of good faith to his fellow partners and this includes a duty to share any benefits which he obtains personally but which emanate from his position as partner or from the use of the firm's business connections. It is probably a moot point whether your partner's activities are connected with his position in the firm, but they are at least likely to affect the energy which he devotes to the firm. Since the duty of good faith is at the heart of any partnership, then as a matter of good practice, he should make a full disclosure of his outside earnings to his partners so that the problem can then be ventilated between you. Legally, it is doubtful whether you could force him to account to you for a share of his profits, but court proceedings for an account are the ultimate possibility. In practice the wisest course would be for all partners to engage in a full and frank discussion in order to agree on some guidelines, before working relationships are affected by this problem.

Q: **I recently joined a firm as a partner. I had previously worked on my own account and had built up substantial goodwill, but I felt that I needed more support and more opportunities for development. The firm was very interested in me and we negotiated an arrangement which seemed to be mutually beneficial. Six months on I have discovered that the accounts which were shown to me by the senior partner misrepresented the firm's financial position, and it looks as though profits this year will be very much lower than was forecast. My partners have not given me straight answers on this, and I feel that I have been seriously misled.**

A: It is doubtful whether a false representation designed to induce a person to become a partner in a firm could ever be given in the ordinary course of the firm's business. That means that any legal liability may only attach to the senior partner who actually discussed the financial position with you (see p 40). As you looked at accounts, however, it is likely that the other partners may be considered to have authorised or ratified the handling of the negotiations, but you may have to establish this.

Your main problem will be to decide whether or not the whole relationship has been so soured that you wish to recoup your losses and withdraw from the partnership. Assuming that you do, you could sue the firm under the general law of contract to recover the capital that you have contributed and to cover yourself against any partnership liabilities. The knock-on effect of bringing such proceedings would be the dissolution of the firm.

Appendix 1

SENSITIVE WORDS AND EXPRESSIONS

The use of a partnership or business name which includes any of the following words and expressions will require the approval of the Secretary of State for Trade and Industry.

Association	Federation	Post Office
Assurance	Foundation	Reassurance
Assurer	Friendly Society	Re-assurer
Authority	Fund	Register
Benevolent	Giro	Registered
Board	Great Britain	Reinsurance
British	Group	Reinsurer
Chamber of Commerce	Holding	Scotland
Chamber of Industry	Industrial & Provident Society	Scottish
Chamber of Trade	Institute	Sheffield
Charter	Institution	Society
Chartered	Insurance	Stock Exchange
Chemist	Insurer	Trade Union
Chemistry	International	Trust
Co-operative	Ireland	United Kingdom
Council	Irish	Wales
England	National	Welsh
English	Patent	
European	Patentee	

The use of a partnership or business name which includes any of the following words and expressions also requires the Secretary of State's approval. A statement that a written request has been made to the relevant body seeking its opinion as to the use of the word or expression together with a copy of any response received will be required.

Word or Expression	Relevant body for persons intending to set up business in England or Wales	Relevant body for persons intending to set up business in Scotland
Apothecary	The Worshipful Society of Apothecaries of London Apothecaries Hall Blackfriars Lane London EC4	The Pharmaceutical Society of Great Britain Law Department 1 Lambeth High Street London SE1 7JN

Word or Expression	Relevant body for persons intending to set up business in England or Wales	Relevant body for persons intending to set up business in Scotland
Breed, Breeder, Breeding	Animal Health lll Division Ministry of Agriculture, Fisheries and Food Tolworth, Surbiton Surrey KT6 7NF	As for England and Wales
Charity, Charitable	Charity Commission Registration Division 57–60 Haymarket London SW1Y 4QX	Scottish Home and Health Department Civil Law and Charities Division St Andrews House Edinburgh EH1 3DE
Contact Lens	General Optical Council 41 Harley Street London W1N 2DJ	As for England and Wales
Dental, Dentistry	General Dental Council 37 Wimpole Street London W1M 8DQ	As for England and Wales
District Nurse, Health Visitor, Midwife, Midwifery, Nurse, Nursing	United Kingdom Central Council for Nursing, Midwifery and Health Visiting 23, Portland Place London W1N 3AF	National Board for Nursing, Midwifery and Health Visiting for Scotland 22 Queen Street Edinburgh EH2 1JX
Health Centre	Department of Health PMC 1C Division Alexander Fleming House Elephant and Castle London SE1 6TE	As for England and Wales
Health Service	Department of Health HS2B Division Eileen House 80–94 Newington Causeway London SE1 6EF	As for England and Wales
Nursing Home	Department of Health Room 604 Eileen House 80–94 Newington Causeway London SE1 6EF	As for England and Wales

Word or Expression	Relevant body for persons intending to set up business in England or Wales	Relevant body for persons intending to set up business in Scotland
Police	Home Office F1 Division Police Department Queen Anne's Gate London SW1H 9AT	Scottish Home and Health Department Police Division Old St Andrews House Edinburgh EH1 3DE
Polytechnic	Department of Education and Science FHE3 Division Elizabeth House York Road London SE1 7PH	As for England and Wales
Pregnancy, Termination, Abortion	Department of Health PMC 2A Division Alexander Fleming House Elephant and Castle London SE1 6TE	As for England and Wales
Royal, Royale, Royalty, King, Queen, Prince, Princess, Windsor, Duke His/Her Majesty	'A' Division (Room 730) Home Office Queen Anne's Gate London SW1H 9AT (if based in England) Welsh Office Cathay's Park Cardiff CF1 3NQ (if based in Wales)	Scottish Home and Health Department Old St Andrews House Edinburgh EH1 3DE
Special School	Department of Education and Science FHE3 Division Elizabeth House York Road London SE1 7PH	As for England and Wales
University	The Privy Council	

The use of certain words in partnership or business names is covered by other legislation and their use may constitute a criminal offence. Some of these words are listed below but the list is not exhaustive. Owners of a business wishing to use any of these words in a name should consider seeking advice from a solicitor and confirmation from the body concerned that the use of the word does not contravene the relevant legislation. It should be noted, however, that the opinion expressed by a particular body is not to be regarded as conclusive.

Word or Expression	Appropriate body
Anzac	Seek advice of Companies House
Architect, Architectural	Architects Registration Council of the United Kingdom 73 Hallum Street London W1N 6EE
Bank, Banker, Banking Deposit	Bank of England Threadneedle Street London EC2R 8AH
*Chiropodist, *Dietician, *Medical Laboratory Technician, *Occupational Therapist, *Orthoptist, *Physiotherapist, *Radiographer, *Remedial Gymnast	Room 77 Department of Health Hannibal House Elephant and Castle London SE1 6TE
*Where preceded by the words Registered, State Registered, State	
Credit Union	The Registry of Friendly Societies 15/17 Great Marlborough Street London W1V 2AX
Dentist, Dental Surgeon, Dental Practitioner	General Dental Council 37 Wimpole Street London W1M 8DQ
Drug, Druggist, Pharmaceutical, Pharmaceutist, Pharmacist, Pharmacy	The Pharmaceutical Society of Great Britain Law Department 1 Lambeth High Street London SE1 7JN
Insurance Broker, Assurance Broker, Re-Insurance Broker, Re-Assurance Broker	Insurance Broker Registration Council 15 St Helens Place London EC3A 6DS
Optician, Opthalmic Optician, Dispensing Optician, Enrolled Optician Registered Optician, Optometrist	General Optical Council 41 Harley Street London W1N 2DJ
Patent Office Patent Agent	IPCD State House 25 Southampton Buildings London WC2A 1AY
Red Cross	Seek advice of Companies House
Veterinary Surgeon, Veterinary, Vet	Royal College of Veterinary Surgeons 32 Belgrave Square London SW1X 8QP

Index